Prosetry Journey

EXPLORING EXPRESSION OF THE HEART

MARIANNE LYON AND GEOFFREY K LEIGH

An Integration of Poetry, Prose, and Prosetry

To **Mary & Frank**

loved me   no matter
your smiles abide in my heart
my poems are for you

And to **Joan & Henry**

Many beliefs expressed
sayings, writings, actions
modeling your individual creativity
and complete commitment
Now   attempting to walk
227 pages
in your shoes

Prologue

By **Prosetry**

We mean some combination
of prose and poetry
in such a way
as to make them
equal contributors
to the expression
you are seeking.

Contents

Chapter One

Open Hearts

As you read this first chapter, consider the following:

Imagine the most meaningful work you could do in your life and
how a person might achieve that kind of work.

Open*
Marianne Lyon

He senses
there must be more
Yearns
Climbs to mountain cave
Flowers brighten
Scent entices
Sun warms
Nobody   caveman
greets him
offers him
bread   honey
He tells him
his eyes have run dry
Nobody
invites him
to expand   unlock chest
live from agape heart
cry from unbarred heart
It is strong
When we close
heart becomes
small
Heart is built
for strength   longevity
Hurtful words
are not about us
Allow them
to fly through

Open to gratitude
Open to joy
When grief is expressed
don't shut awakened heart
Open to
honeysuckle
Open to
jasmine
Open your heart
Open all of you
Open   again
and again

*A found poem from *Nobody and Zahir* by Geoffrey K. Leigh

Nobody and Zahir[1]
Geoffrey K. Leigh

A man lives in the same small village where he was born. He has worked as a carpenter his whole life, and he enjoys both his labors and hometown.

But Zahir no longer experiences fulfillment from his work. He senses there must be more to life. Yet, he doesn't know quite what he's missing.

Not long after becoming aware of his yearning, at least for more contentment, he finds himself in a neighboring town. He goes there to deliver a beautiful wooden bowl he made specifically upon his friend's request.

As they sit and drink tea following the examination of the carving, Zahir shares his desire to find more inner joy beyond his simple work pleasures.

His friend looks at him for a moment, then replies.

"I suggest you go visit the man who lives in the mountain cave. Just follow this road up the hill. You'll see the door on your right near the top."

"Why? What does he do?"

"Do? He grows food nearby or sits and talks to people. I just think you might find a visit fruitful."

Trusting his friend, Zahir decides to talk with the man.

"What's his name?" he asks. "How will I know him?"

"His name? Nobody. And he's the only one who lives in that area. You'll find him."

Zahir thanks his friend, packs his money for the bowl into the rucksack side pocket, and begins his trek up the mountain. Because Zahir walks everywhere, he finds the hike only moderately strenuous.

The white and purple flowers along the road brighten his journey. Their delicate scent entices him as the sun warms his back.

---

1. Originally published in Napa Valley Writers Third Harvest, 2021, Gnarly Vine Press, Napa, CA, pp. 46-53.

Zahir stops and bends down to smell the wildflowers. He begins to wonder if he should take a gift to the man. He forgot to ask his friend if that were customary. His rucksack contains nothing more than a little money and some food. So he decides to pick a bouquet, in case that would be a thoughtful gesture when they meet.

As he approaches the summit, Zahir begins to look for the cave. Somehow, this three-hour walk enervated his body. Finally, he spots an entrance into the hill where a man sits on a stool with eyes shut, his back against a rock surrounding the opening.

The man's hair and beard blend with the nearly white granite. He wears a tan robe and sandals. As Zahir approaches him, the man, without opening his eyes, says, "Hi. Welcome to my home. Would you like to sit for a while?"

"Yes, I would. Thank you, sir. It's a long walk here. Are you Mr. Nobody?"

"Yes, I am Nobody," the man says as he opens his eyes. "And what did you contemplate as you walked here today?"

"Well, I wondered if you would like some flowers?"

"Yes, I'd love them. They have a sweet flavor, especially the purple ones. Do you have other items you would share?"

"I just sold a lovely bowl. I have some money."

"I can't eat money. Do you have anything else?""I have some bread and honey."

"Would you mind sharing half with me?"

"I'd be happy to, sir."

Zahir pulls out his bread and breaks it in half as Nobody goes into his cave. He returns with a gray stone jar and hands it to Zahir, who pours half his honey into it. Nobody smells the sweetness, puts the lid on it, and takes it and the bread inside. He returns and sits down on his padded stool.

"What brings you to my home today, Zahir?"

Zahir's mouth gapes open. "How did you know my name?"

"It was written on the side of the honey bottle," Nobody chuckled.

"Oh, of course," responds Zahir, joining in laughter. "Well, I've been thinking there must be more to life than making things, eating, and sleeping. While I love to create carvings out of beautiful objects from nature, it feels like I'm missing something in life. My wife has died, and my two children moved to the city for work. Now I experience little joy in what I do."

"Did you mourn your wife's death?"

"Oh yes, for many years. It feels like my eyes have run dry."

"Then it is time to expand your chest and develop tears of joy. For such drops are a watering source for the heart."

"My wife was a big heart opener. I'm not sure I know how to expand it any longer."

"How much do you want to open your heart now?"

"As if my life depends on it."

"Good. Because it does."

With that, Nobody reaches out with both hands and touches the visitor's chest. Zahir feels a formidable zap, then falls off the rock onto his side. There he remains for an extended time.

He slowly wakes, pulls back the blanket that now covers him, and looks up to see Nobody sitting on his stool eating bread and honey. Zahir pushes against the ground to raise himself, then slides back onto the rock.

"Wow, I think I must have dozed off. How long was I out?"

"About a day," responds Nobody.

"What? No! That's not possible. I thought it was an hour, or two at the most."

"No. Just about a full day. Want something to eat?"

"Yes, I'm starving." Nobody goes into his cave, returning with some spiced cooked grain and beans along with a cup of water.

The scent from the mixture stimulates Zahir's hunger even further. He gobbles down the food, followed by several gulps of liquid. "My heart feels so full. What did you do?"

"Oh, I just helped you along with your wish. I suggest you go back home and continue your work. When you start to feel your heart close down, give something to someone who needs it. Or tell someone what you appreciate about them. Take this heart-shaped rock with you to remind you of your intention."

"May I give you some money?" asks Zahir.

"No, just keep living from your heart. That's the best gift you can give me."

Zahir thanks Nobody and walks back down the mountain, stopping in his friend's village to thank him.

"Did he help you?" his friend asks.

"Oh yes. He's probably the second greatest gift in my life."

"Fabulous. I'm glad he was helpful," replies his friend, rather sure Zahir's deceased wife remains his greatest gift, at least until now.

Zahir walks back to his village.

Once at home, he continues his carving, which becomes more creative and stunning. People come from extended regions of the country, hearing about his extraordinary creations, the beauty of the wood or stone, and the velvet feel of the surfaces. Some are wooden or stone animals, others carved people, or scenes from the area.

But as Zahir maintains the expansive opening of his chest, the trunk of his body increasingly morphs into a heart shape.

As that transpires, the villager's aversion to him proliferates. They begin to shun him. It becomes increasingly difficult for him to get food, clothes, or other needed supplies. Few people talk with him when he walks through the village.

Zahir decides to move away. He packs up his belongings and carving tools, sells his house, and moves to a distant part of the country, everything he owns stuffed into his cart. The rock Nobody passed on to him gets carefully tucked into his rucksack.

Besides his carvings, he begins to create colorful oversized cloaks to wear.

These hide his body so others will be less afraid.

In this new village, Zahir finds a small green house with a shop in front where he can display his work. He can live in the back with a square opening to watch the shop and a back door to enter or leave his home.

He displays the wooden and stone carvings he makes in the shop with a price sign by each. As people enter, a door creak informs Zahir. He dons his large cloak and comes to the front shop to help them. Hiding his body seems to make it easier for others to interact with him.

As people examine his exotic carvings, they increasingly enter into conversation with Zahir. Customers begin to spend greater amounts of time chatting with him rather than solely focusing on the carvings.

Later, as more people gather in the shop, Zahir brings out carved stools or elegant pillows he has created for people to sit on as they prolong their discussions.

Visitors often ask him for advice about their lives or how they might solve differences with their spouse, friends, and neighbors.

"I don't really know anything about all that. I just know about the heart. If you take what people say personally, you sensitize the organ to collect pain. Such responses do not empathize with the plight of others, but rather internalize the hurt they pass on to you. As people fling cruel words your way, both hearts live in contracted pain.

"Yet, the organ is naturally strong when we don't make it small. If you don't sensitize it to take on hurts from other's words, then it can hold tremendous grief and gigantic love. It is built for strength and longevity. But when we constrict it by taking on the sting and ache passed to us by others, our heart has a more difficult time."

"So how do we avoid taking on such pain? How do we strengthen the heart?" one neighbor asks.

"First, by recognizing that others' hurtful words are not about you, but about them. So don't make the pain yours. Allow the words to fly through without becoming attached to them. Second, open the heart through gratitude. Share appreciations with your spouse, your children and friends. Feel gratitude for the beauty of this land or for some small gift you've received. Grieve fully for a loss or for the pain that exists in the lives of those around you. Then give joy when the grief is fully expressed, once gratitude and love have returned."

The crowds grow as the rainy season diminishes. Zahir and the villagers move to the hillside behind his home, as the shop no longer can contain such large groups.

The fresh air relaxes those attending, and they relish the scent of honeysuckle and jasmine on the hill.

When the sun comes out, Zahir's cloak gets hotter. First, he removes the hood, and people continue their conversations. When he stands up to make a point and the cloak falls open, not a sound occurs. People keep listening and asking questions.

A woman in the front raises her hand. Zahir nods for her to speak.

"I see your heart is so open that it has influenced your body. Could you help us do that, Mr. Heartman? I want my heart to be that big."

Zahir stands still in shock, both at the ease of her question about his visible body shape and her reference to a new name.

"Well, I suppose I could. Although I'm not exactly sure how this happened. But I will help all I can."

People continue to come, sometimes different guests on different days. Many stop in the shop to buy a stool or pillow for sitting on the hill, or a creation because of its beauty.

Since Zahir now spends little time attending to his shop, he puts a sign in front. It reads:

The attendant is not available.
Please take an item you like
and leave a little money in its place.
Thank you. The Management

Zahir enjoys meal preparation, but little time exists most days for that, too. The villagers now bring food to share with him and each other.

As people spend greater time around him, they find themselves happier, more relaxed, more concerned with others, and even, in some cases, healing their own illnesses.

They request more opportunities and time in group conversations with Zahir present.

One day, a man raises his hand. "How do we help our children open their hearts?" he asks.

"Oh, you don't have to worry about teaching children to open their hearts," responds Zahir. "What you pay attention to is avoiding words and behaviors that encourage them to close down their hearts, like most adults already have done."

Another man stands, and Zahir motions for him to speak. "As I focus more on my heart, my wife says my sexual desire has decreased dramatically. While she likes my greater openness, she is not happy about my lack of physical interest. What do you recommend?"

Zahir looks into the man, closes his eyes, and remains on his stool for a few moments. The crowd watches him in silence.

After a time, he opens his eyes.

"Is your wife here with you?" he asks.

"No, she stayed home to prepare more food. She'll be here tomorrow while I stay home to work."

"I suggest you go home, take your wife into your bedroom and both of you remove all clothes. Sit in a comfortable place and take turns telling each other ways that you are grateful for your spouse, at least 10 times each. Afterwards, give each other a big hug. Then allow yourselves to roll around on the floor laughing, loving, kissing, and touching each other. Ask her to report back tomorrow. I suggest you go begin immediately."

The man gets up, thanks Zahir, and leaves.

The next day, a woman in front raises her hand as soon as Zahir welcomes the crowd. He motions for her to share.

"Yesterday, you gave my husband some instructions about our physical connection. I just want to say we had the best sex ever. Thank you!"

"I see," said Zahir. "Could you speculate about why that might have been?"

"I don't know for sure, and who knows if it will work every time. But my guess is that when both our hearts and bodies are open to each other, our physical and energetic connections are greatly amplified. I think my husband got so focused on opening his heart that he left his body behind," laughs his wife. "But I think we are finding our way back to verbally and physically expressing our love."

The crowd applauds at the wife's remarks. Zahir joins the response.

As time passes, the size and frequency of gatherings decrease. Instead, spontaneous conversations and exchanges of gratitude take place all over the village.

As such discussions increase, body shapes began to replicate their hearts.

After some time, Zahir appears normal among his community. He quits wearing cloaks and begins to create heart-designed clothing in bright and lively colors, exaggerating rather than concealing the new body shapes.

Some people come to town and become afraid of the strange-looking residents, disappearing as quickly as they arrive.

Others visit and notice how happily and peacefully the people live. Some relocate to the village, wanting to participate in this intriguing community.

Zahir feels sadness that he couldn't touch the hearts of people who didn't remain. It seemed to him their fear of what they saw overpowered the subtle access to love.

He now spends half his time at the edge of town, wearing his cloak, giving hugs to all who want them, sharing a heartful gift without conditions, as he received.

Heart #1
Marianne Lyon

My heart bids me open her
wants to feel awareness
touch acceptance   hear trust
Always thought acceptance   overrated
awareness   impossible
trust   just for saints
But inquisitive   I ask her
What is wide openness like
A smile instead of a grin
A hug   not a walking away
A hymn   exhaling miracles

Heart #2
Marianne Lyon

I invite my open-heart step outside
We unlatch one   and then another
there's Dad   Mom   Auntie Fran
anxious to tell us of precious portals
they have walked through
some liquid as an ocean
some infinite as Einstein's sky
even heaven's door
when they became angels
for a long string of moments
Deaths door is just threshold
to another and another

Writing Prompts 1

Introduction: These writing prompts are here to stimulate different ways to look at subjects and write about them. You may use one, all, or none of them, of course. The ones that appear attractive to you are an easy way to start. The others that as less appealing may, in the end, provide more creative stimulation. Our suggestion is to try some, at least, that do not immediately look fun or interesting, especially after you have tried some that are.

Best wishes with your writing, and we hope these diverse prompts assist in expanding the way you write or the topics that you use.

1. Think of a favorite folk tale you knew as a child. Fashion a poem from this tale. Does it appear different from the way you saw it as a child when using an alternate format?

2. Write a poem or prose piece to one or both of the anonymous quotes: "The strongest hearts have the most scares."

3. "It's impossible, said pride. It's risky, said experience. It's pointless, said reason. Give it a try, whispers the heart."

4. Imagine the most meaningful work you could do in your life. Write about how a person might achieve that kind of work and what impact it might have on her/his everyday living.

5. Consider how your own heart opens wider. How and when does that happen? Could you create ways for that to happen more often? What is the fear about such experiences? Describe these elements in a short story or extended poem.

6. By prosetry, we mean some combination of prose and poetry.

Write a poem or a prosetry piece about your relationship to a favorite folk tale. What would you include that may not be contained in the original story? How might you integrate your own personal experience with the tale?

7. Spend some time writing in a journal during this next week. See what comes up and how you might express such thoughts and feelings through different literary forms.

CHAPTER TWO

Conversations

As you go through this chapter, consider the following:

If you could communicate or interact with someone who has died, who would you choose and why?

Naked*
Marianne Lyon

In small place I sit
above my eyes   mirror hangs
Want to see   talk to mom

But   inside closet space
Dad appears in bright glass
feel shock   elation

In closed walls
Says   *he loves me   sorry too*
I deeply listen   cry

In this reflected place
his concerned face soon dissolves
evaporates   gone

I sit   slowly   replay
conversation   he said   *there is more*
healing to be done

When I leave cubicle
can hear others thoughts so clear
they know mine as well

Their words come as if
saying them out loud   it's not
natural   so disturbing

Uneasiness hangs
How far will this go   when will
it end   I feel naked

*A found Haiku from *Side Effects* by Geoffrey K. Leigh

Side Effects
Geoffrey K. Leigh

I sit in the room, roughly the space of an oversized closet, trying to relax into a moderately comfortable chair. A mirror hangs slightly above my eyesight, with a dim light underneath my seat. The space appears to be harmless. Yet, I have no clue what the impacts may be from this simple experience.

I searched for over a year to find someone with this kind of setting, where individuals could possibly interact with dead loved ones. The tiny room provides another opportunity in my exploration of consciousness, which adds to my excitement.

Such settings, called psychomanteums, intrigue me. Ever since I read about Moody's research in his book, *Reunions*, I desired such an opportunity.

The investigations that followed Moody's work inspired hope in me, with a large percentage of people reporting contacts. I want to talk with my mother, who passed away a few years earlier. Of course, other relatives could appear; Dad, Grandma Catherine, Grandpa Charles, Uncle Reed, Aunt Hannah, Aunt Marion. But I hope for Mom. Besides the experience, I crave one more connection, a chance to finally say 'good-bye' after her sudden death.

Most mornings, my velvety sheets entice me to remain in bed for dreamy pondering or reading. Earlier today, they couldn't contain me. I was up at first light, inhaling the ocean breeze while shaving and showering, donning the clothes laid out the night before.

I planned a stop at the coffee shop near the Concord BART station en route to the therapist's home. Fortunately, going from Albany to Concord, my travels opposed the busyness of early morning commuters making their way to offices, cubicles, and stores, which allowed me to relax and contemplate the possible encounter with a departed relative.

After disembarking the train, I stopped for a salted caramel latte and bran muffin on my way to the 10:00 appointment. Extra time allowed me to appreciate the aromas billowing from the shops and flowers along the way. Other people scurried down the streets with bags and briefcases, suites, phones, shined shoes, high heels, and coiffed hair. I felt grateful to disrupt my usual routine.

I found the house nine blocks away, introduced myself and followed the therapist into a sitting room, unsure whether the excitement was in the atmosphere or confined to my body.

We talked for a while in a sparsely decorated room and comfortable blue overstuffed chair before introducing me into this dimly lit room. I have seen larger walk-in closets at open houses in high end homes my brother sold.

As five minutes pass, I consider whether this might be a hoax or another failure in a series of glamorous attempts. Suddenly, my father, who passed many years before Mom, appeared in the mirror. I feel shock and elation, hardly able to distinguish such reactions.

To my astonishment, we begin to communicate. But not through traditional verbal exchanges. Some place in my head or body, I knew what he is intending to say and able to express what I want to share.

I'm sorry I wasn't more emotionally available to you. But know that I loved you very much, my father tells me.

Similar to many 20th Century men born from British ancestors, he struggled with emotional expression. He feared it would make me soft and unable to deal with the world of strong males. He tried to help.

But I made it more difficult to trust and express your feelings, he tells me. *I'm here because you know your mother loves you. There is more healing to be done between us.*

He shares more about his love and concern for me. I listen as tears flow down my cheeks.

The interaction lasts about 20 minutes. Then his face dissolves back into the glass following one more *I love you*.

After staring at the mirror and briefly replaying our conversation, I exit the room and sit down to discuss my experience with the therapist.

Oddly, I can hear her thoughts, as had occurred with my father. I know she retains many more questions about my conversation that she's not asking.

I figure it's just a hangover from my interactions with Dad. I pay and thank her for the session.

As I make my way to catch the return train, a headache begins developing. Upon arrival at my apartment, the ache increases dramatically.

Rather than being located in one particular spot, as usually occurs, this one seems to encompass my entire head. The strongest part of the pain seems to occur in the middle of my brain.

My balance remains wobbly and the room begins to spin. I experience nausea, lightheadedness, fever, and blurry vision. I take some aspirin, remove my clothes and fall into the soft sheets.

My inquisitive mind seems unsure what is happening. Yet, I decide to wait before seeing a doctor. Maybe I have contracted something, possibly the flu. With luck, this all will pass quickly. My caressive bedding beckons me, finally falling into a deep slumber.

When I awake the next morning, relief reigns. The nausea has passed and the pain in my head vanished. As I stand, the room no longer spins. The fever and lightheadedness also take their leave.

There remains a type of ringing, but not in either ear. It seems to come from the center of my head, in an odd but not overly obnoxious fashion, as previous ear ringing had been.

I still call in sick. I want to spend the day assessing my experience and any residual effects.

After arising, I shower and dress, eat lightly, and take extra care of myself. My body feels better, yet the ringing continues.

I search the Internet about psychomanteum impacts or after effects.

Similar symptoms come up from tinnitus and brain tumors, but any ringing occurs in the ears or relates to hearing loss rather than a sound emanating from the center of the brain or increased sensitivity.

I google the effects of psychomanteum experiences. People report a decrease in grief, a change in their view of reality, and modify their meaning of life. As I reflected on these items, all appear accurate with me. Yet no one mentions ringing in the brain or increased hearing sensitivity.

While sitting at my desk, considering the search results, my phone rings.

"Hey, Hakeem, how was your experience yesterday? I haven't heard from you," says my dear friend, Sonya.

The physical effects captured my attention. I forgot to call her.

"It was great, except I didn't feel well afterwards. It doesn't seem to be a common outcome, but I felt rather ill after getting home."

I continue on to explain what happened in the room, how joyous I felt to experience such an interaction with Dad, and what happened physically upon my return home. I promise I will check in with her again over the next few days.

I begin to hang up when I become aware she thinks this all may be a hoax.

"No," I said, "it wasn't a hoax, I'm sure."

She responds. "I have no idea why you're saying that."

I decide to let it go.

"OK. Tomorrow's Saturday. Why don't you come over for lunch and we'll talk," I suggest.

She agrees.

After I hang up the phone, I hear the voices of a couple arguing in the next apartment, yet unable to make out their words. I hadn't paid attention to their argument at first. Upon tuning in, increasingly I can hear their words and their thoughts.

Mike says he did not mess around with that guy the other night, when in fact he had. His husband, Steve, accuses him of an affair while hiding his own encounter guilt.

The two guys were likable, but I contain no desire to know such intimate information. I certainly want to avoid involving myself in the couple's conflict.

The next day, Sonya comes over for lunch. We talk more about the experience along with my excitement to hold a conversation with Dad and grateful for his loving message. We spend time discussing the caring connection.

Finally, she asks me, "When are you going to talk about your ability to read my thoughts?"

I'm in shock. "How did you know?" I ask.

She responds telepathically.

Because I can read yours! I wondered why you asked me the question about the session being a hoax on the phone the other day when I hadn't verbalized anything about that. But now I know. And apparently, I also can hear what you're thinking.

Stunned, I stare at her, unsure what to say.

I'm shocked. I had no idea you could do this.

I couldn't until today, replies Sonya. *I've never experienced this until part way through our conversation.*

The two of us continue our discussion, sometimes verbally, sometimes solely through our thoughts. Soon our exchange centers around how vulnerable we feel when we can't keep anything secret from the other.

At the same time, there exists a hint of relief and some sense of authenticity. But for both of us, the primary concern focuses on our defenselessness.

The next afternoon, I hear a knock at my front door. When I open it, Mike stands there with a plate of cookies.

"I bringing these over as an apology for our loud argument the other day. Hope it wasn't too obnoxious. We were kind of upset, but we've sorted out our differences finally. We'll try not to do that again."

"The cookies aren't necessary. You guys weren't that loud."

I pause, looking more intently at the plate.

"Are they chocolate chip?"

"Yeah. You told me some time ago you loved chocolate."

"Oh, well, I guess you were kind of loud. I'll keep them," I say with a brief laugh. "Glad you two are doing better."

"Oh, so you know about the affair too, eh?" Mike blurted out.

"What? No, I don't know anything about an affair."

"Um, sorry. I mean. Wait, you didn't say that out loud?" Mike asked.

"Say what? An affair? No."

"I could've sworn you said that. I was sure I heard you say that."

Can you tell that I'm trying to hide what I heard? I ask telepathically.

Yes, I can, replied Mike similarly.

Have you always been able to hear people's inner thoughts? When did your ability to do so begin?

"Oh . . . . well . . . . just now," responds Mike verbally.

"Geez, I don't know what's going on. My friend started to hear my thoughts the other day, too. Can Steve do the same thing?"

"No, I don't think so. He hasn't said anything about it, and he didn't know what I was thinking or hiding the other day when we had the fight," he responded.

"Well, let me know if this continues, will you? I'm curious how this happened."

"Yeah, sure." With that, Mike walked his astonished look back to his apartment.

Wow, I thought to myself, *how far will this go? Where will it end? What are the implications of this spreading everywhere?*

My uneasiness increases.

Over the next week, things continue to change.

In a meeting with Jerry, my boss, his concerns about the new ad campaign I've been heading up come to me clearly.

My curiosity arises as to how this occurs in others.

When a colleague, Tom, comes in to ask about the project, his desire to find out about it so he might undermine me comes across loud and clear. I want to let go of this mind talk; an overwhelming task with such blaring chatter.

My sense of defenseless soars when both of them tell me what I'm thinking, given the power my boss has over my job and the rivalry that has developed with my colleague.

At the same time, Tom and I no longer try to pretend we aren't jealous of each other's accomplishments.

Even my assistant, Rachel, and our group secretary, Pam, begin to hear what others are thinking. This only increases both the vulnerability and initial conflict among the working group.

I tell Rachel and Pam I'm not feeling well and need to go home. I hope they couldn't tell that I'm lying. But then, they probably know anyway, given the tentativeness in my voice.

Upon returning home, I loosen my tie and shirt, then collapse onto the couch, wanting to avoid all that's occurring around me. I wonder if I'm causing such changes, with no idea of how to stop it from happening.

As I relax and begin to doze, my father appears again.

You seem distraught. What's wrong? he asks telepathically.

I can hear what everyone's thinking. If I focus my attention on any particular person, their thoughts come as if saying them out loud. And now they can hear my thoughts. It's not natural and very disturbing, I respond mentally. We continue our conversation in that fashion.

Don't you want to know what people are thinking? he asks.

Well, yea . . . . except this is more information than I want. It feels intrusive. Like I'm seeing them naked.

You are, he says. *What's wrong with that?*

It's . . . it's too much information. And I don't want them to know what I'm thinking. I don't want to be naked to them.

Oh, so you want to use verbal language so you can lie to them?

What do you mean? I tell people the truth.

Like coming home sick? my father asks.

I feel a massive knot developing in my stomach.

Well, sometimes I have to. I just make up a little story to help me get out of things.

Right. To lie.

But mostly I tell the truth.

Do you say everything you're thinking?

Well, no . . . . no, not all the time.

Right. Verbal language was invented for lying and keeping secrets, not for sharing the truth. I didn't realize that until I died. But after you get over the shock of being naked, it's nice to let go of all the protections for your lies and secrets. I think it's one of the reasons I feel much lighter.

But you don't have a body either.

OK, there is that. But even beyond the weight of a body, I feel lighter not having to hide anything.

Well, I'm not ready for that. I'm not ready to be naked with my thoughts.

Then focus solely on verbal interactions. Your ability will fade once again as you focus on the hiding.

Really? I'll be cured?

Yes. You'll regain your defenses and quit hearing their naked thoughts.

Oh, good. I thought I was going to be this way the rest of my life. That scared me.

I feel my body relax and my father fades away. I doze again for a while. When I awake, I feel more normal.

The next day, as I stop for my coffee, I can't hear what anyone was thinking. At the office, it's the same thing.

A sigh of relief escapes from my mouth as I gathered my mail at Pam's desk, having no idea what she was thinking.

"Anything wrong?" she asks.

I give her a wide smile as I let out another sigh.

"No, thanks. It's all good today, and hopefully tomorrow too."

I turn and enter my office, happy to feel conventional again.

Yet, my father's words began to haunt me. The freedom and ease reappear for a moment, providing a brief sense of relief.

What if he's correct?

Maybe I should try to maintain the skill. He implies I can reclaim it. I feel I should.

Yes, maybe someday. But not today.

Dad came to me
Marianne Lyon

Dreamed I was blazing
through open field
split open with sunlight
inside a Van Gough
mustard   knee high
oaks bend in prayer
crystal staircase   ahead
I start to ascend
white light chases place
free of shadows
ancestors begin to take shape
move like water
in their original stream

Dad turns toward me
looks like a Blake Poem
"Father, Father!
Where are you going?"
I feel myself move to him
kiss his forehead
polyphony of memories surge
rest in my mind   vibrate my ribs
scenes twist my heart backward
to faintest imprint of what they were

I suddenly understand
his struggles as mine
but the shine in corner of his eyes

glow that life must
pass through difficulties
to achieve any morsel of joy
a man at ease now
his smile contains everything

I breathe his breath
we become one piece.

Writing Prompts 2

1. Write about something in your life that had a serious impact on you. Try writing it with a different process or outcome. You have the freedom to create when you allow that to happen.

2. How might that event have been different? Either for better or worse, depending on how you want to view it differently.

3. Now take the same issue and write about it in an alternate format (if you used prose, try writing about it using poetry or the reverse).

4. If you could communicate or interact with someone who has died, who would you choose? Write about that in a form you don't usually rely on to express your deepest thoughts. You might even try "automatic writing," which is simply writing for a while without thinking about it. Just see what comes out after 15-20 minutes of writing as fast as you can.

5. Imagine a person who cannot hide anything she/he thinks. What might that be like for both the person and for others around that individual? Describe what that would be like as you create such a scenario.

6. Other than not wearing clothing or having people know what you are thinking, what other aspect in your life would make you feel most vulnerable? Write about what a person might experience if they became naked in that way.

Chapter Three

Gardens

As you read the poems and short story in this chapter, consider the following:

What magical process has attracted you?
If none, why do you think that is?

Nasturtiums
Marianne Lyon

Come with me
into my nasturtium garden
faces   fiery palate of color
round leaves bounce

like china-tea plates
that dutifully held cookies
for my baby dolls
each summer afternoon

Come with me
spend some time
with nasturtiums   abundant
story keepers

listening   feeling   seeing
them bathed in afternoon rain
like soothing murmur   with promise
of sun blanketing soaked grass

Let them fasten your gaze
Yoke sacred communion
Give them your eyes
rayed with smile lines

Notice how they dance on whimsical breeze
full of seed   full of possibilities
Listen   a good report comes from

satisfied hummingbird

Come with me
into my garden of nasturtiums   tangoing
Get lost in their rustle-talk
watch sun transform them into light

The Garden
Geoffrey K. Leigh

I walk out to appraise my herb garden with a mug of steaming coffee. The vessel provides toasty comfort through my hands. Rows of shoots burst out, reach for sunshine with undisguised determination to flourish, nutrified from last year's mulch and winter rains.

I notice my impatience for their maturation, anxious to explore novel health remedies. I take a deep breath, invite my body to soften, feel into the earth as I amble along on this first short-sleeve day of spring.

"Looks as if it'll be an excellent crop," says Pablo, as he strolls up the next row. "Glad you added those additional beds last fall?"

"Oh, yes. Plenty of work, but it'll be worth it. The St. John's wort and ginseng are coming along nicely. I'm excited to infuse the lavender flowers."

"What type of oil have you decided to use?" Pablo asks.

"Avocado oil. It helps with inflammation."

"So how are you feeling today? The depression getting any worse?"

I stare at Pablo. His face exhibits innocence as he asks whether the verbal blade he effortlessly inserted into my emotional body still hurts.

"I'm fine!" I snap.

"OK, sorry. I'm just concerned since you got off your meds."

"You know I hate how they make me feel," I tell him.

I soften my voice, realizing the intensity of my hasty response.

"Does the regular biking help, if I may ask?"

"I think it does," I tell him. "It seems to give me more energy, too."

I take a breath, wanting to recapture a calm and affable atmosphere.

"How about a hike later today?" asks Pablo. "Maybe we'll discover new wildflowers. The mustard sure is exploding in the vineyards."

"Yeah. That would be lovely."

I want to go with Pablo. Yet today, I feel lethargic. I'd hoped the garden would energize me. Yet, his inquisition dampens any enthusiasm.

"Actually, how about a hike tomorrow? I'd like to work in the garden today."

"Alright, that's fine by me. I'll get some snacks for us while at the store later," responds Pablo, his voice flat. "I'm going to fix an omelet for breakfast. Want one?"

"That would be wonderful. I'll be in momentarily to help."

"Great. I'll get started."

He returns to the house while I wander further to check the chamomile. The coffee aroma induces another sip, followed by a breath that relaxes my body. Still, my inner darkness looms, unaltered by this morning's sunshine.

I grab my phone, turn on the drip system with my new app as I continue down the beds, to assess any potential problems with emitters. Returning several rows over, I watch, making sure plants will get the water they will need as temperatures rise. The garden appears healthy, my inner space remains malnourished. I go inside, hoping Pablo completed his inquisition.

Together, we make scrumptious omelets accompanied by toast and more coffee. We discuss what we need from the market and which hike we'll take tomorrow. After breakfast, he leaves for the store while I launder the kitchen.

I return to the patio, seeking more fresh air and sunshine. I decide to pull out my meditation cushions. Maybe sitting will enliven my inner environment.

The resulting tranquility helps, but only to hint at a dim light in the distance, an interior sunrise that never materializes further.

The next three weeks bring scattered rainfall and abundant sunshine. The plants thrive. When not at my winery job, I care for and begin to harvest the early herbs for the Farmer's Market on Thursday.

Upon arrival at the market, the herbs get organized. I share a table with Darius, who sells jars of creative preserves and local honey in addition to enjoyable conversation. Pablo creates tags with herb names, along with a list of medicinal qualities.

His contributions make my work easier, but his efforts supply minimal light to my inner murkiness. So I again camouflage myself as a cheery extrovert for my interaction with customers.

By the time we clean up and prepare to drive back home, my body feels depleted of remaining resources. My contracted muscles persist, creating a challenge for deep inhales. The cannonball size weight in my chest adds to my sense of demoralization. A thick, smokey haze prevents any illumination to foster core viability.

The next morning at breakfast, Pablo leans in, places his hand on mine and inquires further.

"You still seem pretty down. Are you sure you shouldn't begin your meds again?"

I hear the softness in his voice. But my interpretation of being wrong on top of my deflated mood and body inflames me as I remove my hand.

"God damn it, Pablo. I'm trying my best. You know I hate the foggy mental state and numbness the meds produce. They make me feel like a fuckin' zombie. I'm eating a balanced diet, exercising almost every day, using some herbs regularly, and will soon include others with the infused oil. I'm feeling better, actually, even if you don't notice. Just give me more time. It'll work its way out, I'm sure."

I notice the heat in my face, soreness in my throat, from my elevated tone.

"You don't have to yell at me. If you were truly feeling better, you wouldn't become so enraged every time I ask about it," he responds.

"Well, you constantly nag me. It's going to take time. Just leave it be."

Heat reddens my cheeks. I know he's right. That pisses me off even more. Feeling wrong and broken amplifies my discouragement. My eyes feel hot when I look at him.

Pablo takes a long inhale, blowing the air out slowly through his rounded lips. His eyes focus on his open palms. He then turns to me.

"Look. I'm sorry. I know you're working hard at this. I love you. I want you to feel better. I get frustrated not being able to help. It's difficult for me to live with too. I just wish there were something more I could do to improve your mood."

I take a deep breath, slowly exhaling as I look at my loving and frustrated husband.

"I know I'm not easy. I hate feeling this way. But it seems I'm slowly finding a way out of this darkness. It's just taking longer than I'd hoped. My other herbs are about ready, and I'll have a full array by the first of the month. Give me another six weeks on this regimen. If I don't begin to feel a whole lot better by then, I'll restart the meds."

I suspire once again, then I continue.

"I'll try not to get so upset when you ask how I'm doing. I love you, too, and I realize this is no way to show it. But I want to get a hold of this through natural remedies if I can. Alright?"

"Alright. I won't ask, *if* you'll give me some indication of how you're doing. Will you agree to initiate an update each week if I agree not to ask?"

"Yes. That's reasonable. Very fair." I give him a hug and kiss his cheek. "I'm going to work in the garden for a while."

Several days later, I instigate the infusion of lavender flowers in avocado oil, then begin to process the ginseng and St. John's wort.

I continue to eat a balanced diet, including only natural sugars in fruit while incorporating daily exercise of biking or fast-paced walks. Meditation practices commence daily. They provide some uplift. My body begins to feel more expansive, relaxed.

At the same time, the cannonball black hole remains in my chest, a 24 pounder rather than the larger 32 pound caliber I wielded previously.

The following week, Pablo goes out of town, traveling down state to attend a seminar. Now alone in the house, I decide to undertake an inner journey, a possibility we discussed before he left.

I find my container of dried psilocybin mushrooms, cultivated for our use. I pulverize several in a grinder, making it easy to weigh and mix into spiced tea. A touch of honey sweetens the taste.

The cup containing the tea bag and honey sit next to the small container of mushrooms. I proceed to the patio, pull out my cushions for a sit. I want to incorporate a hallowed underpinning to my exploration.

As I breathe in, I relax my thoughts and my body. I continue to focus on my breath, allowing whatever comes into my mind to float away. A balloon full of thoughts drifts outside my mind.

After a twenty minute meditation, my emotional state elevates moderately. I return to the kitchen, pour warm water over the tea bag and honey, remove the tea bag and add the mushrooms, stir, and consume it.

About thirty minutes in, effects begin to occur. I sit on the cushions again, pay attention to my body as my eyes survey the garden.

Healthy plants transform the beds into a lush, verdant wave, that oscillates in the breeze. The increasing nausea informs me of more mushroom influence. I begin slow deep breaths to calm my stomach, still reviewing my abundant garden.

Gradually, I rise and remove my shoes. I want to feel the earth embrace my feet. Fascinating scrunch sounds reach my ears as I walk down the rows.

With each type of herb, I bend down to catch whatever scent is emitted, taste the plant, relish the flavors erupting in my mouth. Afterwards, a new urge moves me to another scent, a different flavor. Some taste tart or tangy, others spicy or zesty. The lemon mint fills my mouth with freshness that I savor for an extended time.

As I wander through the garden, leaves and flowers begin to sparkle. My eyes relax as different colors emerge around the herbs. Each type produce its own hue and texture.

The plants appear increasingly diverse, finally visible in their essential form. I meticulously examine each variety, get to know its virginal appearance and sense of how it impacts my physical and emotional bodies.

Interacting with the foliage in a renewed manner gives me a deeper appreciation of every plant. After a while, a desire arises to transition from the detail to a panoramic perspective.

The cushions call me once again. I return to consider a holistic view.

The entire garden dances in the warm breeze, light and airy, yet grounded deeply in the earth. A harmonious herb cantata progressively severs the silence.

I delight in my evolving inner environment. The cannonball begins to shrink, my muscles relax, light strengthens as the haze evaporates with increasing warmth, like late morning mist evaporating around the vineyards.

Yet, something remains missing. An element I want. Need, in fact. But, what to ask for when I lack any awareness of what's absent?

I stay with the pleasure of my increasingly tranquil body. The ability to breath effortlessly. The lightness of my being. The transformation delights me, even with the nagging question of what else may contribute to the alterations. How could there be more?

I decide to ask the mushrooms, or the universe, or whatever may provide insight. What else is missing? What else addresses my need?

I sit with these internal questions, open my eyes, and look out at the colorful warbling herbs, now seemingly untethered to the earth.

Abruptly, I feel an enormous ball of light developing in my abdomen. The ball's warmth increases, as does its familiarity, in some way known before.

As it expands, it feels extraordinarily loving. The kind of imagined affection when I think of being held in the arms of my mother, adoring her little baby boy.

Yet, even that image does not begin to describe the unconditional acceptance permeating me. Peace and intimacy I don't remember experiencing or even imagining spreads inside me. It feels as real and authentic as anything previously encountered. Joy spills out of open eyes and runs down my cheeks, heart pounding, taking my breath away. I sit with the encounter, afraid the feelings will fade with any movement.

My eyes focus again on the dancing herbs, as if they celebrate this exploration. Demonstrating my inner situation with their swaying movements, they invite the outer me to stir. I suspire slowly, requiring oxygen, yet fear the disruption of my rapturous delight that exhilarates every cell.

Gradually, I move my arms, then legs, which beg for a stretch. My breath flows steadily. I pay attention to my ecstatic body with each movement. A desire for undistracted motion, while maintaining my connection to this inner incitement.

The cannonball gradually dissolves, the darkness obliterates. Light and love remain the only elements I encounter.

Sometime into my fourth hour of this journey, the mushroom effects begin to fade. The inner light remains.

I rise to walk among the herbs, paying attention to the ball of love while thanking them for their delightful enthusiasm. I stroll in gratitude around the entire garden, still attuned to my inner sensations. I begin to trust the shift may remain.

A realization emerges: I constantly look outside myself for what evident-ly exists inside all along.

Pablo returns two days later.

"You're looking and acting different, my love. What's happened to you while I've been away?"

I share my experience while he listens quietly. I tell about my mood elevation, followed by the dramatic emergence of the loving light inside me and the unique lighting of the herbs.

"And how are you now? Do you still feel any depression?"

"It shows up. It's not like the depression disappears completely. But now, a fissure exists when it invites me in, enough space to make a choice. I know my habit of easily collapsing into depression. At the same time, I can expand the internal ball of light, which gives me an essential alternative."

"Do you think it will last? Will you quit doing the other things you thought would help?"

"I hope this option lasts. Feels like it will. Yet I have to choose the light, to invite the expansion. And I won't quit the other components that helped me open to this encounter. It's a system that seems to work collaboratively. But the loving light is the linchpin."

The following Thursday at the market, I need little camouflage to interact with customers. Joy fills me in sharing the herbs, now wrapped with purple ribbon instead of a bland twist tie.

A man walks up and asks if I have lavender oil. Surprisingly, I notice a brown spot energetically hovering around his liver. I hand him a bottle of the oil. After he pays, the turmeric glows, as it did in the garden. Upon recovery from my additional shock, I hand him a bag.

"Here, take this. It, too, may be useful."

He looks at me for a moment, says thanks and leaves.

Another customer walks up and wants some thyme and chamomile. I see the rosemary illuminate. I hand her the two requested, then throw in the bonus herb, suggesting she might include this with her meals.

The lighting effect doesn't happen with all my customers, and I may never know if the additional herbs benefit those people who receive them. They often appear lighter upon their return.

But I inexorably find this way of helping others nurtures my own health and contributes radiance to my inner world.

Light-filled*
Marianne Lyon

I
walk out
appraise herb garden

Shoots
burst   reach
for morning's sunshine

Still
unaffected
inner darkness looms

Rise
remove shoes
feel earth's embrace

Self
wanders   flowers
begin shimmering sparkle

Garden
dances   cantata
duets with silence

Delight
bursts inside
my inner environment

Query
infinite universe
for her insight

Suddenly
I feel
enormous light ball

Luminous
invites me
make a choice

*A found Hay(Ha)Ku from *The Garden* by Geoffrey Leigh

Writing Prompts 3

1. Identify a magical process that has attracted you. What would it look like, feel like? How would it change your life or an imaginary character in some significant way?

2. Now write about it in a form (a short story, a poem, a newspaper article, a report) that is most challenging to you. See if it brings out anything more or unusual in the process.

3. Spend some time looking at nature around you. How might you view it differently than you have in the past? Take an alternative outlook than you have previously. Then write about that experience, expressing both your perspective and the feelings associated with that.

4. When was the last time someone really upset you? What was going on inside and what might you have ignored in the process? Write some prosetry about an alternative view and how that might be helpful to you in the future.

5. Consider the following quote from the last poem. Take a moment to inquire, then write about your experience and any insights that came from such a query.:

Query
infinite universe
for her insight

CHAPTER FOUR

Searchers

As you read this chapter, consider the following:

What is something in life you were not able to achieve and
how might a person make that possible?

Why look for God?
Marianne Lyon

Look for the one looking for God
but then Why look at all?
He is not lost
He is right here -Rumi

I circle dawn lake
stop at brilliant light patch
scented Pinecones drop

From ceiling of trees
blackbirds preen on branches
sagging over tarn

Am drawn to clearing
cannot walk by   breathe deeper
lose urge to go on

Is God right here
He may be   dear Rumi
but still I feel adrift

He gently whispers
look for unmarked path
feel your breathing unravel

Still hear breeze on lake
a song that blackbirds imitate
I walk off matey footpath

Off familiar stretch
silence walks with me
wish I was a bird

A black bird   not lost
cheeping long vowels
trilling   contented

In Search Of The Oracle
Geoffrey K. Leigh

Turning age 18 and graduating from high school in the same month became Elisa's rite of passage out of her mother's church. She tried to make it her church. Time and again she tried.

Her mother, Amara, raised in a strong Italian Catholic tradition, deeply embedded herself into her religion. Thus, the white wooden framed three bedroom, two bath home had the same scent as every Catholic Church Elisa entered. If she closed her eyes as she sat on the squashy tan living room couch, her nose couldn't tell which structure she was in. She could distinguish by the soft cushion under her butt, but not the odor.

Brown wooden crosses appeared on the wall in several strategic locations, including above Elisa's bed. As she got older, Elisa figured it was an unsubtle reminder of what might happen to her if she rejected Mom's religion.

Amara apparently hoped that giving her daughter a name which meant "pledged to God" would encourage her to become a nun. If Elisa didn't follow that path, at least maybe she would be inclined to forge a solid Catholic foundation in her own family.

Her daughter knew early, however, that she wanted none of the cloistered life. The Catholic foundation hadn't worked up to now either. Elisa felt certain it never would manifest. At least it seemed like a 'never' from her 18 year-old view.

Her religious experiences reinforced the sense that conflicting organizations developed an increased hardening of the categories. The limits she encountered were rock solid, maybe even petrified, allowing little movement and variation.

Yet, a connection to the Divine was important to her. She just couldn't find it through the rules and teachings of the church. Why would she want to be a part of an institution where women were second class citizens? Men were the Popes, except for one apparent error centuries ago. Men were the Cardinals, men were the Priests. Men were in charge of everything, which was fine with her. Let them have the institution. If a Supreme Being existed, she would find her own connection. One more flowing and open.

As she continued to consider her mother's path, that same sinking, sickening feeling would fill her chest and gut. Women seem to be the baby bearers, and she wasn't sure she wanted to bring a baby into such an institution. She wanted to walk a different road.

Elisa's younger brother, Gabriel, seemed more committed to their mother's church, and who wouldn't with a name like that. With her dad gone, no one knew where, Elisa was outnumbered.

But in that religious struggle, she somehow discovered a hidden strength. Something deep inside would buttress her stand, creating a solid internal feeling, yet unable to detect its genesis. In those times, this felt like the true meaning for the name of the first book in the Bible. She only desired to access this strength as easily as her mom could manifest her holy book.

This deep, strong feeling would appear, seemingly at random times. But Elisa was unable to count on it in a consistent fashion. Her New Life Resolution on high school graduation day was to find someone who could help her identify and figure out how to keep that source as a constant in her life.

The one place such strength and even clarity showed up came from playing music. Her dad left his trumpet when he abandoned the family. Elisa felt no loyalty to him. But she loved that old silver plated Getzen. And it was readily available.

Amara agreed to pay for lessons if she practiced the instrument every day. She even threw in a free mute to make it easier for others to hear her practice those first rough years of odd notes, off key, missed scale exercises. Especially on weekends when her mom was working at home. A closed door and muted trumpet helped sustain what remained of family sanity.

Elisa got a job at a local music store during high school. She saved every penny she could and bought a used electric keyboard using her employee discount. Her mom bought accompanying earphones as a gift to herself. Elisa began taking piano instead of trumpet lessons.

Elisa, through her music, found the freedom she could not find anywhere else in her life. Especially not in her mom's religious institution.

"You going to stay at home and attend college here in Reno?" asked Gabriel one day.

"Hell no! I'm going to head south."

"You sure Mom will support that?" A doubtful look emerged on Gabriel's face.

"Yea, we've already negotiated that. I get to go away to school, and I'll leave her church intact. She seemed to think it was a fair deal," responded Elisa with a laugh.

Her gratitude for choice increased as she drove out of Reno to attend the other state university in Las Vegas. She used this opportunity to take world religion and philosophy classes while majoring in her true love, music.

Her ability to play piano provided major assistance in her initial attempts at composition. It remained as rough as the first couple of years learning her instruments. She loved jazz, especially the works of Miles, Coltrane, and Herbie. She idolized Keith Jarrett's ability to effortlessly play both classical and jazz genres.

It was now within this musical space where she felt most liberated. She could let go within a creative expanse that felt virtually limitless, never ending. This was the place of spirit, freedom, love, and peace among what many called 'chaos.'

Yet, even in the spacious grandeur of improvisational riffs, there remained a confinement of her being that she could not abolish, could not dissolve. This was at least a means for greater flow, creativity, and expression in her life, limited only by her imagination and skill.

Las Vegas provided opportunities to play with others outside the safety of academia and test her skills. It was not a perfect transition. Yet, it provided essential experience with pick-up groups, a means to earn money with street performance, and improv at clubs after turning 21.

Following college, Elisa moved to the Bay Area, where there were more opportunities to connect with other musicians, develop different styles, and explore alternative religious groups.

Initially, hats or cases laid out on the sidewalk. She played for those ambling by, hoping to touch them with her soft, poignant melodies mixed with a few wild riffs. She rotated between her battery powered Roland and her old reliable Getzen. Elisa would venture to harmonize with the style of clothes, looks on faces, sparkle or sadness in the eyes, even one's coiffure on people passing down the street. And she did not ignore the apparent insolvent or derelict, back up against the building and asking for change. They too would elicit some new tune or sound that might improve their day.

It was a natural setting to meet other troubadours, listen to anything new they might offer, create some clue of what was emerging when not playing the old favorites.

Once the street music was over, she spent nights in any clubs she could afford, using her meager earnings to listen to new groups if she didn't just sit outside and take in the sounds for free.

As she was leaving her street performance one evening, two men came up behind Elisa. The first guy grabbed her, one hand over her moth, another chocking her neck. She tried to twist out, then kick a leg. But the guy behind her seized both arms and threw her hard against the cement, scratching her face and hands. The men snatched her wallet and money from her case, then ran.

She looked up to see them as a warm liquid flowed into his eyes, stinging sharply. She wiped away the red liquid from her face.

She had no clue who they were. They looked like so many on the streets in the later evenings; old clothes, worn down shoes, jeans and a sloppy shirt, one white, one puke green with a hole in the back, both wearing black caps.

Not sure she would make much of a witness with no facial recognition.

She lay on the sidewalk for a few moments, still holding on to her trumpet that now had a creased bell. At least she would have the appearance of an authentic street musician with scratches on the horn that would match her forehead.

Gabriel called the next day to see if he could come visit. "How you doin,' sis?"

Elisa hesitated, then said, "Fine, thanks. How are you?"

"Well, thinking of coming down to see you and a couple of friends. Could I crash at your pad? It'd be nice to spend some time with you, too."

"Yea, that'd be fine. When?"

"This weekend. Say, you sound kind of sad. Everything OK?"

"Yeah. Just got mugged last night and lost all the money I had on me. It was a pretty good evening too, damn it!"

"You alright? Did you go to the hospital? Concussions are easy to get, you know."

There was a sudden alarm and protection in Gabriel's voice that always felt supportive to Elisa.

"I'll be fine. See you Friday?"

"Yeah, probably early afternoon. And we may need to go get you checked."

"I'm fine. See you then."

Elisa enjoyed the weekend with her brother, taking her focus off he loss of money and sore head.

The following week, she found a supplemental job at a local coffee shop, serving freshly brewed java, lattes, often with soy or almond milk, accompanied by a muffin or sweet bread. She enjoyed watching the people, deciding in her head what music they might want to hear.

Sometimes she would switch up tunes on the play list when her boss was away. She tried to figure out what music might cheer up the grumpy old man in the corner when he would sit at his usual table and nurse his 12 ounce black coffee for a good two hours. He would snort at anyone who entered 'his space' or complain about something in the shop.

One day, when the manager was out running errands, she took the coffee urn over and asked, "would you like me to heat up your coffee?"

"How much?" gruffed the dark eyed old man, his faded white t-shirt slightly above the v-neck blue and red plaid shirt that covered the band of his torn jeans.

"Store treat, today only."

"Yea, sure. Not like I don't buy a lot anyway."

Elisa poured a full cup, rendering a smile as she did so, wondering if there was anything she could do to elicit a similar response from this constant customer. She found the exercise an interesting failed experiment. Still, it was worth a try.

When not working at the shop, Elisa played music at her favorite location (daytime only from now on), or listened to groups at bars.

She also began to explore non-traditional spiritual groups that were less familiar to her. A fellow street musician told her about a gathering one evening to learn about the Enneagram, a tool that can help unravel distortions in the way people see themselves. The presentation intrigued her. But she didn't have the money to attend a workshop. Instead, she went to a local shop and bought a book on the subject that might give her some insights.

She also read about near-death experiences where people wander into the light after leaving their bodies. On the other hand, she desired to find some assistance while she still could breathe, fire synapses, and circulate blood.

She began to visit Buddhist and Sufi gatherings to get a sense of whether they might be a useful expansion of her spiritual world. She hoped for some magical guru. A magnetic attraction to someone who could help her with the inner darkness. Some enlightened being who could show her the way to the light while still living.

Elisa increasingly focused on making connections with other musicians.

She wanted to land a gig that would pay better than her street music.

Eventually, a friend invited her to try out with a group that was integrating American jazz with Middle Eastern fusion. Her combination of piano and trumpet helped with the introduction. Her performance got her the job.

This group provided a new creative challenge. It expanded her experience with evolving segments of the music world. After rehearsing long hours, the new group began playing in more avant garde clubs with extraordinary response, leading to their first CD.

Based on this success, an opportunity emerged to play internationally. The offer provided a chance to travel, experience other cultures, see more of the world than the limited view perpetuated in her early Nevada life or even in the more diverse Bay Area.

The group first received an offer to appear at the Bahrain Jazz Festival, followed by a two week gig at the Coda Jazz Lounge in Manama, Bahrain. Elisa knew it was in the Arabian Gulf. But she would not have been able to place it on an unmarked map.

This gave her a chance to visit the Middle East, an important influence on their music. Manama allowed greater tolerance of women's dress, although some precautions were needed about covering knees and shoulders. Given that three of the seven group members were female, such lenient considerations were essential. At the same time, this provided an occasion to explore an interesting part of the Middle East where people were more broad-minded than Saudi Arabia.

While in college, Elisa began to study esotericism, books by Sartre, Teilhard de Chardin, Rumi, a book on the Kabbalah, the Tibetan Book of the Dead, and teachings of Confucius. She had read them all. She decided to take only two small books with her on this journey; one by Rumi and a book about Confucius to continue her explorations while traveling. Given she had few clothes, she felt compelled to drag the books along.

While music was her love and vocation, exploring a connection to the divine that some reported, even with the near-death research, became her primary exploration.

The 21 hour flight was long and tedious. Only two stops along the way. But October was a good time to leave the coming rains in the Bay Area and to visit Bahrain when the weather begins to cool off.

Band members cherished the opportunity to play a whole set at the festival. Several thousand attended the event, full of excitement. Elisa was fascinated to hear other jazz groups from Europe, South Africa, India, as well as Bahrain. She had no idea that this small Middle Eastern country had such a love of this musical style. And while attendees were mostly familiar with traditional jazz, the avant garde and mix of Middle Eastern fusion created the greatest enthusiasm.

After the festival, they played six nights a week at a local establishment. The stage at the jazz lounge was tight with seven players, including a piano.

Elisa had never been in a bar so filled with smoke, both from cigarettes and hookahs. There were small round tables with comfortable swivel chairs filled by couples and small groups. Two larger tables overflowed with people near the back. The room included soft, colorful, indirect lighting with little on the walls to distract attention away from the music.

People were appreciative and friendly. They often wanted to meet band members and encouraged diverse tunes.

Sophia, the stunning, thin, red headed singer, was particularly popular and often hit upon by the men. This made it easier for Elisa to hide in the background. She got a marginal share of attention. Still too much for her.

During the serene days after a late sleep, Elisa had time to read, see some historical sights, enjoy life in the city. She spent time in a local coffee shop with a good book and her choice of Italian, Turkish, or Arabic coffee. She sometimes chose the latter, as it burst open with the taste of cardamom. It also included that nutty, sweet anise aroma, almost spicy, but not quite cinnamon or clove. She relished the flavors. But the pungent smell incensed her back to Amara's church. Such rememory created an unpleasant taste in her mouth.

She sat in the shop one day, reading a book by Rumi. A woman approached her table.

"Mind if I sit here?" the woman inquired, obviously a local from her black hair, olive skin, English accent, and mix of western and middle eastern dress.

Elisa looked up at her beautiful smile and offered her the seat with an extension of her hand.

"You live here?" asked Elisa.

"*Ayuwa*. Born and raised in this neighborhood. Are you American?"

"Oh yes," said Elisa. "I'm Elisa. Born and raised in the States, and enjoying my time here for the moment."

"Hi. I'm Fadima."

"Nice to meet you, Fadima."

"It appears you like Rumi," responds Fadima as she scoots her chair closer to the table. "Do you know much about him?"

"Yes, I have read a book about him and love his poetry. That's about all."

"Are you familiar with other famous Sufis, like Hafiz or Ibn 'Arabi?"

"I know Hafiz's poems. He's awesome too. Never heard of the other one."

"He was also a Sufi philosopher and poet, but born in Spain in the 12th Century, about the same time as Rumi."

"Interesting. Don't know his poetry."

"He's known more for his philosophy. He's a very interesting scholar who argued, much like Rumi and Hafiz, that no separation exists between humans and God."

"Oh my, that's very different from my Christian training. Tell me more."

"When people understand the lack of separation, they begin the path of ultimate oneness. The one who decides to walk in this oneness pursues the true reality and responds to God's longing to be known. The search within for this reality of oneness causes one to be reunited with God, as well as increased self-consciousness."

"Wow, that sounds interesting. In ways, these are issues I have wanted to explore further."

"Would you like to attend a lecture about him tomorrow afternoon at the Isa Cultural Center? It's free and open to the public. There also will be some Sufi music and dancing."

"Ah, I don't know. I guess. Are you going?"

"*Ayuwa*, yes. My family is very involved in the Sufi tradition. When I saw the book you were reading, I thought you may have such an interest."

Elisa attended the lecture and dance with Fadima, which turned out to be enlightening and enjoyable. The dervish whirlers swirled like tops with white outfits pushing outward as if they were holding them up, assisting their twirls.

The audience seemed more interested in the music and dancing. Yet Elisa was intrigued by the lecture. There was talk of wisdom from different prophets, most shared by Christianity, Judaism, and Islam. The speaker discussed the idea that God's essence is seen in the existent human being, as God is the object and human beings the mirrors.

Elisa had never heard of such ideas. They seeped deeply within her that evening and over the next few weeks.

She didn't see Fadima after that evening. She never failed to remember this coincidental meeting.

The next day, as Elisa was out walking, she passed by a jewelry store that had some very intriguing rings in the window. Elisa went inside and discovered puzzle rings, interconnecting ring bands. It was designed as a type of mechanical puzzle, that creates a lovely and unique pattern when properly integrated. The shopkeeper described them as symbols of the thought and effort that helps keep friendship or marriage bonds strong.

For Elisa, it felt like the commitment to find that strong bond to the divine. She bought a four band sterling silver ring, the least expensive yet still intriguing. It became a commitment and reminder to herself of her search for such a divine connection.

She was not supportive of the second class role for women here. Yet, as she swirled the ring, it felt like a reminder of other gifts garnered in this locality. Gifts like meeting Fadima, attending the lecture and dervish dance, and divergent ideas to consider.

As their gig in Bahrain came to a close, the group landed another in Delhi, followed by participation in the Clarence Jazz Festival in Mumbai. With little discussion, the group voted unanimously to be part of both opportunities.

It took several days to get visas. Then they all flew to New Delhi.

Given they had 10 days before their gig started, Elisa and Sophia decided to spend a few days in Nepal, visiting Pokhara and Kathmandu.

While they didn't plan on hiking the Himalayas, they wanted to see them up close. Elisa also wanted to see the Swayambhunath Temple and the Boudhanath Stupa, both important to Buddhists, as well as the Garden of Dreams in central Kathmandu. It was a wonderful visit and felt like a magical experience, even among the less than tidy cities and countryside.

While meditating in the garden, a practice she learned from her Bay Area Tibetan Buddhists, Elisa kept feeling into the mirror concept Fadima shared with her and the lecturer discussed further. She wondered with hope. Was she shining her mirror?

The two young women returned to Delhi to find the others partying with some local musicians. They later showed the girls some of the local hot spots they had visited.

The city was very busy, often with a whiff of cumin or coriander intermingled with decomposing meat or cow dung, the metro system was new and convenient, especially for people on a limited budget. Elisa fell in love with the savory food and wonderful scents from spices she knew but did not have all around her; the turmeric, cumin, saffron, and masala. They excited her digestive juices and her sense of smell. She also became addicted to the chai tea served on many street corners.

The group's agent arranged for them to play six weeks, rotating between three different clubs. They offered a variety of music, usually some variation of jazz. Their diverse music attracted a following wherever they went. Elisa enjoyed the reappearing familiar faces and the support locals provided.

As their club time ended in Delhi, the group had several days to hang out in India. All wanted to see the Taj Mahal in Agra on their way to Mumbai. They had not made a final decision as to when they would leave.

With a little time on her hands, Elisa went for a walk in the neighborhood around their hotel. A local bookstore caught her eye. The store contained many worn books in the window with titles in several different languages. She recognized those in English and some in other European languages, at least two in Arabic, which she had come to discern, and many in Hindi.

Then she noticed an interesting poster in the window about a Satsang with an Indian guru, Acharya Prashant. She went inside and inquired with the shop owner about this man whose picture was on the poster. His photo mesmerized her.

The man stopped looking through books, searched deeply into Elisa's eyes, then said. "He is the most crystal clear teacher I know. If his photo catches you, I suggest you attend."

"Yes, it does. Is it hard to get in?"

"No. I know a friend who works with him. He will get you in, and it does not cost a lot. It is a one day meeting tomorrow from 1:00-7:00. Well worth your time. And this one will be in English, so it will be easy for you. Meet my friend here at the store by 12:30."

"I'll be here," responded Elisa.

The retreat was in the area, quite close and convenient. She felt her body hair standing on end with excitement for another chance meeting with a teacher. She noticed a confirmation feeling in her chest that it was a salient event to attend as she walked out of the shop carrying her most recent purchase, *The Upanishads*.

On her way back to the hotel, Elisa passed by a women's clothing store. She had purchased very little while on her trip, besides this new book, an Ibn 'Arabi book and puzzle ring while in Bahrain. Suddenly, she had the urge to purchase a piece of clothing to celebrate her trip to India.

She walked in and wandered through the shop. Many different possibilities of women's clothing caught her eye. A green floral print kurti tunic with solid green pants magnetically pulled her.

"You would look stunning in that," said a woman approaching her from behind. "It goes nicely with your brown skin tone and dark hair color. I think you would look lovely wearing this in any country."

Elisa turned to look at the older Indian woman approaching. Her brown wrinkles suggest streaks of wisdom with white contrasting teeth,. Her red and gold silk saree and blouse brought out her trim waist and beautiful figure.

At first it seemed like a great sales pitch, one she could hear at Macy's or Nordstrom in any city in the States. As she looked deeper into the woman's eyes, it felt more sincere.

"Would you like to try it on?" continued the mysterious sales clerk. "Women don't buy as much green these days. So I could give it to you for a good price. Would you be paying in rupees or American dollars?"

"It would be rupees. But I need to know the equivalent in dollars, as I'm still not so great at converting the amounts."

The woman looked closely at Elisa's figure, then found two outfits close to her size.

"You try them on, and I'll see what I can do for a price," she said.

Elisa took them into the dressing room. The first one fit superbly. It was love at first fit, stimulating desire to wear it at the retreat. But she still worried about the cost. She changed back into her clothes, then took the dresses back to the clerk.

"Did one fit you well?" the clerk asked.

"Yes, this one is lovely," handing it to the woman. "And what would it cost me?"

The woman looked down at her numbers again, then back up at Elisa.

"Your first trip to India?" she asked.

"Yes."

"Well, it usually costs 4200 rupees, or about $51.00 American dollars. With our sale, I could give it to you for half price, or about $25.50. But for your first visit to India, and I suspect on a budget, I will give this to you for 1800 rupees, or about $22.00. Would that make it possible for you?"

Elisa could hardly hide her shock. "Yes!" she said. "That would be wonderful. I'll take it."

"As you should," said the woman. "It will be perfectly lovely on you, and you will glow with the matching color of your heart chakra."

"What?" Elisa asked. "What do you mean?"

"Do you know about the human chakras?"

"I've heard of them, but I don't know much." "My dear, green is the color of the heart chakra. It will assist you to open yours even more than it is now. That's another reason I thought it would be perfect for you."

The clerk opened her arms, and Elisa fell into a loving hug with this amazingly wonderful stranger. The woman wrapped up the clothing, gathered the rupees from the open hand, and Elisa began her return to the hotel.

As she walked past the restaurant next to the hotel, she saw her friends eating dinner. They waved, then went in to join them, though she felt physically satisfied from her magical travels.

Elisa told the others about the one day gathering she wanted to attend. Rather than travel separately, the others decided to stay in the city an extra day. Then all would travel together to Agra. Elisa thanked them, sharing how important this felt to her and how grateful she was for their flexibility.

During the retreat, there were two meditations that allowed Elisa to relax further with each one. In between the meditations, Guru Prashant talked about the essence of love and the 'lover' people have been missing.

This lover is our true nature. Once tasted by our being, it can become one with each of us. With it, his type of love brings courage and completeness. It shatters misconceptions and brings each person to rest within love in its truest form.

He also made reference to the famous quote by Confucius, 'No matter where you go, there you are.' The question this guru asked is what type of you do you want to travel with? What type of you do you want to show up wherever you are?

As Elisa sat in this forum, her joyful and hopeful tears were frequently at her eyes edge, sometimes slipping onto her cheeks. Gratefully, she had tissues in her bag. She felt both exhilarated and tired, from work, travels, and the emotional strain journeys can have on a person.

At the same time, she felt exuberant hearing the 'crystal clear' words of this man, translating ancient ideas to her current life. It was a fairly intimate gathering. That felt even more endearing to this seeker.

At the end of the gathering, Elisa bought his book, *The Lover You Have Been Missing,* signed by this guru with oceans of love swimming just behind his pupils. He thanked her and suggested she spend more time here some day. While her current plans were to return to the Bay Area with a trip back to see her family in Reno, she also knew she wanted to see this man again.

Their visit to the stunning Taj Mahal was delightful. Their music at the Mumbai jazz festival seemed greatly appreciated in a country long influenced by middle eastern music and the love of jazz. Yet, Elisa was ready to return home.

On her flight back, as her friends talked, slept, watched movies, and drank, Elisa finished Guru Prashant's book. There was a truth to his words that seemed familiar.

As she dozed after devouring this read, she remembered a quote by T. S. Eliot that she loved from her literature class at UNLV. She was not sure she remembered it exactly. But it was something like, 'we shall not cease from exploration, and the end of all our exploring will be to arrive where we started and know the place for the first time.'

As she pondered this eloquent saying, she viewed it a little differently after her experiences.

Upon our arrival back to where we started, she thought, *we will know the place from a fresh view. That's very correct. Yet, as I focus on the idea of love is our essence, it feels more like a remembering what has been lost. It feels like something I knew before, and when absent, knew it was missing. I just wasn't sure what it was that was missing. And I guess in that way, maybe I know it from a larger perspective, restorative experiences, with more wisdom regarding its importance. Maybe in that way, I do know it for the first time within this perspective.*

This provided a softening of the categories she was seeking. A personal connection not based on external barriers, petrified rules and external authorities who appeared entrenched in power and money more than a personal flow with the divine.

As she fell asleep, it felt to her that the connection, the Oracle, had been found. But it was not someone outside herself. All of her experiences and guides simply pointed her in the right direction.

Found Poem*
Marianne Lyon

Wants to find
Connection to Divine
Discovers   hidden strength
But unable to detect it genesis
Clarity shows up with music
She feels liberated
a creative expanse
Limitless
Never ending place
of spirit
Freedom
Love
Peace among chaos
Yet in spacious grandeur
Confinement
Remains
Hopes for magical guru
To dissolve inner darkness
Connection again becomes
her exploration
Rumi   Hafiz
instruct
*"No separation between
God and Humans"
We shall not cease from
Exploration
And at the end
We will arrive where we started"*

The oracle has been found

Not outside

But within

*A found poem from *In Search of the Oracle* By Geoffrey K. Leigh

Writing Prompts 4

1. Pick an outcome in life you were not able to achieve. Write about that through a person's struggle that brought about success.

2. Write about your own path as it relates to spiritual, religious, or metaphysical experiences, even if in opposition to such aspects of life. Include experiences and ideas that feel most important to you as well as elements that you would want to do differently.

3. Think about your ideal exploration in the area of spirituality or religion. Write what that would look like if you could live a life exactly as you choose with what you know now.

4. Consider an experience or interaction that felt magical, wondrous, or serendipitous. If you can't think of one that happened, write about one you wished you had or would like to have in the future.

5. Imagine a person who sees something magical about at least one experience each day. How would that impact a life?

6. How would you show a magical aspect in your writing without telling or saying that directly?

CHAPTER FIVE

Gifts

As you read the short story and poems in this chapter, consider the following:

How has love impacted your life?

Gift of Love*
Marianne Lyon

Though we may speak with bravest fire
incensed-place   pulpit pontificates
And have the gift to all inspire
repent   reborn   be saved
And have not love, our words are vain
Hallelujah   Hallelujah   Hallelujah
As sounding brass, and hopeless gain

Though we may give all we possess
not fancy words just   enloven ones
And striving so our love profess
"thanks for being here for me"   "I'm sorry"
But not be given by love within
sparkling beings   asleep we are
The profit soon turns strangely thin.

Come, Spirit, come, our hearts control
endear   cherish   make complete one another
Our spirits long to be made whole
Remember   remember the forgotten deep within
Let inward love guide every deed
Gift ourselves   others   embrace our infinite love
By this we worship, and are freed
Our only earth-place option   our only heavenly choice

Italics – Gift of Love – Traditional English Song
*A found poem from *A Surprise Gift* by Geoffrey K. Leigh

A Surprise Gift[1]
Geoffrey K. Leigh

"Don't leave your bike in the driveway. Your mom may not see it when she backs out and could wreck it!" shouts Lance, Ronnie's father and church pastor. "You need to take better care of your possessions or you won't have anything to play with. Money doesn't just magically appear, young man," reminds his dad for the seventeen millionth time as he returns to the house.

Ronnie walks over, moves his bike the necessary six inches to get it off the driveway. He starts to breathe again. His lanky body quivers as he hustles back to his basketball game, his thumbs between his fingers as he approaches the basket. He wipes away his tears as he grabs the ball and brings it up into one arm, determined to beat the national championship team.

He misses an easy layup, then a jump shot. He takes another breath as he looks toward the basket for a moment. Each time he misses, he grabs the rebound and shoots again, with more relaxed determination. He wipes his brow of sweat with his arm.

He's warm still, during an uncommon heat wave occurring this early Nebraska winter. Ronnie wants to finish what may be his last game of the year.

He makes his next shot.

Stevie and Mikey, his two younger brothers, emerge from the open garage.

"We wanna play too. How about four horses?" asks Stevie.

"In a few minutes," responds Ronnie. "I'm almost finished with my

---

1. Originally published in Napa Valley Writers Third Harvest, 2021, Gnarly Vine Press, Napa, CA, pp. 61-68.

championship game."

"What game? You're playing all by yourself," says Stevie.

"No, it's a game. You just can't see the other players."

Stevie and Mikey stand there with mouths gapping open. Mikey, age 5, squints to see who else might be there, just in case his oldest brother is being serious.

Ronnie makes the winning basket and begins to cheer, arms high in the air.

His father comes out of the garage and tells them to get into the house to take baths.

"You need to be clean for church tomorrow."

"But dad, I don't want to go. Besides, we're starting our final game with good weather."

Lance walks over and slaps his oldest son across the face, Ronnie's hand coming up to sooth his red cheek as he scowls at his father.

"Don't you ever say that about church again. Jesus is the most important person in our lives, and church is the place we learn to love and obey him. Once you are Born Again, you'll know these things and receive salvation."

The boys look at each other, then down at the ground. Lance grabs Stevie and Mikey by their arms and jerks them towards him.

"And don't you two start acting stupid like your brother, if you want Jesus to love you!"

The three boys walk towards the house, eyes down, faces sullen. Lance follows on Ronnie's heels.

Once inside, the boys go upstairs to their bedrooms, hearing tub water running.

"Tilly will be out shortly," says Millie, their mother. "But don't go far. You need to get in there and get all clean for Jesus. Kimie's already finished, so you'll be next, Ronnie."

The boys go into their rooms looking for jammies to put on after their bath. Ronnie lies down on his bed to read until his turn.

But he mostly thinks about church and how much he dislikes it. He sits there so long while the congregation sings, his dad preaches, more singing, more preaching. Ronnie tries to ignore it all.

He enjoys the last part when everyone cheers Hallelujah. Then the whole church thing is over.

"KIMIE, CALL 9-1-1, NOW!" shouts Millie. "Tell them we need an ambulance at this address."

Ronnie jumps off his bed and rushes down. "What's the matter, Mom?"

"There's something wrong with your dad. Go outside and show in the medics!"

Millie kneels by Lance, as he groans and holds his left arm with his other hand, rolling around on the floor. Ronnie stares at his dad's flushed face, then goes outside. He looks up and down the street, anxiously awaiting any approaching vehicle with a reassuring siren.

The ambulance arrives and a man and woman jump out. They grab the stretcher out of the back, then follow Ronnie, who's running towards the front door.

Once inside, the man talks with Millie and asks all sorts of questions. The woman kneels next to Lance, checking his heart, pulse, and breathing. After a rapid assessment, they carefully put Lance on the stretcher, roll him outside. Millie and family follow. They roll the stretcher into the back of the vehicle.

"OK, we'll call ahead. You get there as quickly as you can, safely. He'll be in the emergency area," says the woman sitting next to Lance. The man heads for the driver's door.

With doors closed and sirens at full blast, the ambulance rushes away.

"Kimie, glad you're here. You watch the kids. I'm going to the hospital. I'll call you as soon as I know anything. No use all of us being there with nothing but impatience."

"Mom, I want to go too," pleads Ronnie. "Maybe I can help you with something."

"OK, Ronnie. But we need to go now."

They both dash to the garage. Ronnie pushes the door button, then gets into the van. Millie backs out the van, shifts gears, and rushes towards the hospital. Her head remains forward, her eyes fill with moisture.

"He'll be OK, Mom. I'm sure. He's not that old. And he's strong," says Ronnie.

Millie looks at him, tears streaming down her cheeks.

"Thanks, Ronnie. Glad you're here."

Relief fills Ronnie sitting next to Mom, despite the mixed feelings he has about his father.

"There's a space, close to the entrance," says Ronnie.

Millie pulls in and slams on the brakes.

Ronnie knows it isn't a good time to say anything. But inside he smiles about this race-car side of Mom. Never seen her drive so fast. They scurry into the Emergency Room, then spot the information counter.

"We're here to see Lance Hardas, please. The ambulance would've brought him in a few minutes ago."

"Ah, yes. He's in with the emergency doctor now. Just take a seat, and I'll point you out when the doctor's free."

Millie and Ronnie find two seats by themselves in the intimate waiting area. Silence and the scent of disinfectant remain their primary companions.

A woman in the corner attempts to console her child. Millie grabs Ronnie's hand as the tissue in her other hand wipes the moisture on her face.

"Really, Mom. I think he's gonna be OK."

Ronnie leans his head onto his mom's shoulder, hoping his comments show concern for Dad. The two sit there for some time, Ronnnie now upright. Millie picks up a *Vogue* and stares at the cover, never opening the magazine.

"Excuse me, Mrs. Hardas?"

Millie and Ronnie look up to see a tall, thin woman with dark hair and intense eyes, in a white lab coat. A stethoscope caresses her neck.

"Are you Mrs. Hardas?"

"Yes, I am."

"Hi. I'm Dr. Simpkins. Your husband's doing pretty well. But he's had a serious heart attack caused by a blockage in the left anterior descending artery. This can be very dangerous. I think he should undergo an operation immediately. Time is of the essence with such blockages. I'd like you to talk with the nurse at the window and take care of the paperwork. With your permission, I'm going back to prep your husband for surgery."

Millie's eyes water again and stretches her arm around Ronnie's shoulders. As much for support as concern.

"Yes, . . . um, . . . of course! I'll go see the nurse right now. Will he be alright?"

"There's a good chance, given that we got him here so quickly. He seems healthy otherwise. The EKG confirms our suspicion. So we need to get him in right away. Unless there are any questions, I'll talk with you immediately after surgery."

"No. Please, do what you think's best," replies Millie softly.

With that, the doctor disappears behind the swinging doors.

After completing the paperwork, Millie returns to her seat and takes out her phone. She calls Kimie to let her know what's happening and that they won't be home anytime soon. Kimie sounds calm, her voice flat.

Ronnie sympathizes with her, sharing her anger about their 'Jesus loving, heavy handed' father. Kimie, the oldest child, and Ronnie, the oldest son, seem to get the brunt of their father's fury.

Now Ronnie's with his mom, where he feels safest. But he also worries that Jesus will punish him because he lacks sincere love for his dad. He feels more guilt than concern about his father surviving the surgery.

Ronnie reads several articles in the available *Sports Illustrated*, sleeps until his neck hurts, then watches his mother doze intermittently. Finally, Ronnie softly nudges his mom when the doctor returns. She opens her eyes and sits up straight.

"So, we're finished with the surgery, and your husband did well. It was a little touch and go for a short time. But he seems to be resting now. His vitals are stable. We'll want to keep him here for a few more days. It's getting rather late, and I suspect he'll sleep the remainder of the night from the meds. I suggest you go home and get some sleep yourselves. Come back to see him in the morning."

"Thank you so much, Dr. Simpkins. We really appreciate all you've done for him."

"You're very welcome. I'm just happy we got to him early."

Millie takes Ronnie's hand as they go outside, locate the van and drive home. Apparently they left his race car mom in the waiting room.

Upon arrival, they find the house quiet and dark. Ronnie goes into the kitchen, searching for food. Millie follows and pulls out some leftovers. She heats them up. The two sit down for a late snack.

Ronnie's too tired for conversation. Upon finishing, he gets up, puts his dishes in the sink, and walks back to his mom.

"Told you he was going to be OK, Mom. I'll see you in the morning."

"Love you, Ronnie. Thanks for being with me tonight."

"Sure, Mom. Love you too."

Ronnie leans in for another hug.

The next few days are busy, as the family visits Lance and cleans up the house for his return.

After his dad gets home, Ronnie notices a quieter and softer man. But he figures the 'preacher' is just recovering his strength and will show up again any time now.

Several days after leaving the hospital, Lance and Millie have a chance to talk while the kids are in school. Lance breaks the silence.

"I had an astonishing experience while in surgery."

"What happened, dear?"

"Well, I found myself hovering over the operating table. Then I saw this tunnel of light off to my right, and I followed it. It felt really good as I moved upwards. When I emerged from it, there was a man who had long dark hair, a dark beard, and was dressed in white with a bright glow about him. I was shocked.

"Then he told me, 'It's not your time yet. You have work to do, and your family needs you.' I asked him, 'What do I need to do?' As he looked at me, love flowed from his eyes and said, 'People need to know the truth. You focus on a Supreme Being primarily about rules and punishment. But what about love?

"'Do you feel that?' he asked. I could feel this overwhelming affection and acceptance that was all around and inside my body. 'Yes,' I said. 'What is that?' He looked at me and smiled, 'That's who you are. That's what you are made of. It's your gift to each other when you're in touch with it and share it. Love doesn't just originate in the Divine or someone else. It's the core of each of us.

"I want you to go back and share this message with your family and your congregation. But not just with your words. Show it by how you live your life, treat other people, and respect the earth.'

"I couldn't believe that after studying the scriptures in seminary, I'd never really heard or focused on such a message. But it also was difficult to return, to leave the immense love I felt."

"Wow, that's incredible. What are you going to do?" asks Millie, her eyes tearing up.

"I don't know. But I know I can't keep living and preaching the way I've been doing."

Over the next few days, family members notice not only Lance's slower pace, but also his softer voice and manner. Others start to observe a difference too.

In church that next Sunday, the assistant pastor gives a sermon on compassion. Lance talks with him after and compliments him on his remarks rather than criticizing something he did wrong or missed, as he typically did in the past. The minister stares at him for a moment, mouth half open, then thanks him.

As they walk out of the church, Lance takes Millie's hand for the first time Ronnie ever remembers. He points this out to Kimie as their parents walk ahead of them. Kimie gives him an odd look. They shrug their shoulders, then climb into the van.

Later in the week, the family makes preparations for Ronnie's birthday. Presents get wrapped and put out on an overstuffed chair. With the food on the table, everyone sits down for a dinner Millie prepared at Ronnie's request.

During the meal, Lance asks, "Why can't kids remember past birthdays?"

Everyone looks at Lance with shock. Ronnie never remembers him ever attempting to tell a joke.

Stevie finally replies. "I don't know, why Daddy?"

"Because they're too focused on the present."

Lance begins to laugh, as does Mikey, Stevie and Tilly. Millie, Kimie, and Ronnie look at the three kids, then Lance in wonderment. Eventually, they all laugh, as much at the kids as the joke.

That night, Stevie brings Lance the Bible as they gather for the birthday celebration. Instead of his usual birthday passage, Lance opens the book to a different section and begins to read.

"Love one another as I have loved you. I'm not sure this passage has ever had so much meaning for me. Someday, I'll tell you about an experience I had during my surgery. But for now, let me just tell you, all of you, that I'm sorry. I'm sorry I've been so rough on you. I'm sorry I haven't focused more on this passage and the way we should be with each other. Kimie and Ronnie, I'm especially sorry I've been hardest on the two of you.

"From now on, I want to show you my love rather than my hand. For I realize that Jesus may have gotten angry, but he never hit a child. And I won't either from now on. I promise that to you. So tonight, rather than reading about another birth, I'd like each of us to share what we most appreciate about Ronnie. Then he can open his presents."

As Ronnie surveys the silent room, he sees red eyes all around. Finally, Ronnie speaks up.

"Sounds great Dad! And maybe another birthday joke. One that's funnier this time?" he says with a chuckle.

Lance gets up and walks over to him. Ronnie leans back, nervous his dad may strike him. Instead, with tears in his eyes, Lance kneels down and gives him a hug.

Ronnie's greatest desire for his birthday was to get a brand new baseball mitt. But that was before he had any idea that a more loving father was an option.

Ode to a Paradox
Marianne Lyon

Rumi says   *everything has to do*
with loving and not loving

I ask why gaping hearts break
why we impale each other
I don't know   anyone who says
they fathom proof is posturing
avoiding this enigma   this anomaly
that lives with   inside all of us

this morning I am wangled
stinging surge eddies around
I crave it   fear it
yesterday it arrived in effusive costume
of wonder   tomorrow will it don
thunderclouds of grief

outside maple leaves belly laugh
with morning waft   through open window
neighbor plays   entertains Bach's
Jesu Joy   resonance waltzes
through me   I imagine animated leaves
awaiting another measure of blissful sound

Friends   I have no preachment to offer
no rubbish on subject of life   loving
but as I puzzle over the *everything* notion
what if all is like music   or maybe just

orotund breeze waiting for hands

waiting for hearts to abandon   dance

unfurl our foliage into sonorous measures

of paradox living   of paradox loving

Writing Prompts 5

1. How has love impacted your life? Is there more joy or sorrow? Try writing a piece that includes both aspects of love and sorrow. How might you share your ideas and experiences with others?

2. Maybe rather than beginning with the written word, you might draw, find or take a photograph that could simulate a written piece.

3. Having written one piece about love, choose a different format to write another. If the first is a poem, practice writing much of the same idea as prose or even a short story or flash fiction (500-1,000 words max).

4. Choose a love song. Use it as a vehicle to write a poem or use the song to write a letter to the composer. Examples might be: Make You Feel My Love (Bob Dylan), Feels Like Home (Bonnie Raitt), All You Need Is Love (The Beatles), Love Me Tender (Elvis), or At Last (Etta James).

5. Write a short story or poem about "A day someone surprised you." Maybe a memory will emerge. Or you might want to create a day with that "someone" from your imagination.

6. Is there anything in our lives we could change that would make us more loving people? Begin to write about this and see where it leads you.

CHAPTER SIX

Membering

As you read the pieces in this chapter, consider the following:

Is there a dream you have had that also impacted your life?

One Sunshine Morning
Marianne Lyon

I awake inside a dream   her liquid voice
lilts a childhood song inside my heart

You are my sunshine   she croons
"I want to feel your warm grin," she pleads

"I have forgotten how to laugh   giggle
twirl a polka   tickle under a chin," I say

She mists away   but *My only sunshine* walks me
through my day   limping along with boredom

I hear   *you make me happy,*
when skies are grey   you'll never know dear

how much I love you   and I ask myself

What have I done with my sunshine
Where is it hiding   Don't know how it happens

but I start to mouth those twinkling words
start to excavate my closeted singing voice

my lips part   feel a warm crease on either side
maybe I could sing   illuminate my neighbor's face

maybe tomorrow   I'll sing to him who wears
a dark whole of loneliness like a shroud

Remembering
Geoffrey K. Leigh

Without a clue about time in the morning, I awaken from my dream. Yet not quite. It's that place just over the threshold from the dichotomous world. A region of physicality I know so well, where I cling to structure while struggling with doubt.

Yet this dream, like few others, draws me back, wanting to return. I luxuriate in the comfort of my sheets while I simultaneously experience the common early morning urge to urinate.

I retract the covers, still wanting to seize that dreamy world. Pressured by the physical prompt, I find the floor with my feet, grateful for the ability to stumble into the bathroom without a light.

Upon eliminating my distraction, I return to bed, hoping to slip across into my previous dream presence. It's not like I can ever will myself into such an experience, no matter how strong the desire. Yet, even to hang out in the memory of that place is sometimes a gift. I feel into the alluring existence of the symbolic.

My alarm startles me, confirming that I will not be able to spend more time here. I've agreed to meet my friend and intimate ally, Rachel, for coffee this morning.

I return my feet to the floor, shower, put on my cherished purple shirt, jeans, and worn sandals. I walk down to our favorite hangout.

For a change, I reach there first. I find our preferred table in the corner, an easy setting to converse without including others. Upon her arrival, we share a sweet embrace. She holds the table as it is my turn to get our usual.

"So, how's it going," she asks as I return, placing her coffee in front of her.

She bends to take in the steamy aroma. I take my seat. Soft classical music, probably one of Beethoven's sonatas, plays in the background.

"Well, and a bit unnerving."

Rachel tilts her head.

"What's going on?" she asks with both her voice and eyes.

"I had an interesting dream this morning that still tugs at me. I so desire to renew the sensation I experienced there."

Rachel lowers her cup to the table.

"OK, now you've got my attention. Want to share?"

"Sure. Of course I can only convey the essence of what I remember.

"I was lying on a mattress in some unfamiliar otherwise stark room. My body felt more like an illuminated energetic figure. That's the way people experienced each other in this place. I was sensing that breach in my core. That spot where I am most alone and lonely, that empty black hole. Several people were nearby, and one said telepathically to others, 'Let's help him experience our support.' The next thing I knew, I sensed an ethereal body snuggling up behind, cradling my being, energetic arms wrapped around me. The figure stayed there for some time, then backed off. I cherished the sustenance such support provided.

"Next, a group of them were sharing different possibilities to give me embodied support. I could hear the conversation. But I couldn't make out their words. I was in one of those dreams from which I never wanted to awaken."

"Well, for my sake, I'm glad you did!" chuckles Rachel softly.

She looks into my eyes with that gentle, loving way she has that helps me taste her total presence and support.

"What are you experiencing now after going through the physical motions of getting up and coming to meet me?"

"On the way over, I was thinking about what my granddaughter told me some time ago. She said something like, 'What if our dreams are our reality, and our reality is really our dreams?' This was one of those dreams I wish were my reality. I treasure the experience. At that moment, the cavity in my core was filled. I felt whole. Now I am aware of the black hole again. I want to go back over that threshold."

Rachel looks at me as she does when she is processing some helpful idea to share in just the perfect manner. I give her time to gather her thoughts, figure out the best way to express them. She reaches over, placing her hand atop mine.

"But there have been times when you have felt that hole filled. You remember the meditation you shared with me about a year ago? And it was not the first time you felt it. But you were aware of a light or fire. I don't recall exactly your term. But something about a burning light in your core. And the hole had disappeared. Or rather filled with the light. Do you remember what you said about that experience?"

"No, not exactly. That's one reason our connection is such an important relationship for me. We help each other remember those important times."

"You said, 'I always want to live from my core outward with this light burning brightly to guide my way.'"

"Damn! That's right. I do remember saying that."

Rachel looks deeply into my eyes.

"And where's that light now?" she asks supportively as an ally can do.

The tears begin to slip over my bottom eyelids. I sit back, lower my head and close my eyes, feeling deep into myself.

It does not take long for me to experience that light, when I remember to connect to it. I realize, once again, that it is never far away. Then I forget. And then I remember again. And in that place, I finally feel enough.

I open my eyes, still filled with the liquid release, raise my head and with all my heart, say, "Thank you!"

She smiles that ally smile of love and says, "Always. And at this moment, I wonder if that was the purpose of your dream? Maybe even to know the light can be there without anyone cradling you energetically."

"Yes, reminding me I can call in the light myself?"

I notice my gratitude and delight.

"You are such a joy! I think you may be right. And . . . I wonder, Rachel, if there really is a threshold separating these two places . . . or even separating us, when I relax and remember."

Awake*
Marianne Lyon

Awake
from a dream
yet not quite
this place
over threshold
this place
draws me back
I luxuriate
a gift
want to remain
where
energetic arms
wrap around
never want to awake
from
this place
where
dark hole disappears
core is filled
with
burning
light
can this place be
here right now
inside memory
and
when I remember
and

remember again

what if

dreams

are reality

what if

dreams

are real

* A found poem from *Remembering* by Geoffrey K. Leigh

Writing Prompts 6

1. Write about a dream you once had. How would you describe it?
   What did it feel like? What were you left with when you awoke?

2. Write about a dream as a metaphor. Use it as an idea or tool rather
   than focusing on it as a reality or something specific.

3. One possibility is to write about the meaning or interpretation of
   a dream. What impressions came up for you? If you were every
   part of the dream, what would each part mean to you?

4. Choose one or both of the following quotes about a dream and
   write to the author. Carl Sandberg said, "Nothing happens unless
   we dream first." Emily Bronte said, "I love the silent hour of night,
   for blissful dreams may then arise, revealing to my charmed sight,
   what may not bless my waking eyes."

5. A "found poem" is one that is created using only words, phrases,
   or quotations that have been selected and rearranged from another text. Revisit Remembering and write your own found poem.

6. Have you thought about an idea that started as prose, then turned
   into a poem? If not, maybe try writing the idea in poetic form.
   Afterwards, write the same story as prose. Is it any different than
   what you anticipated in the beginning? Maybe try the process
   with another idea for a story.

CHAPTER SEVEN

Not Far

As you read this chapter, consider the following:

What does the phrase, 'you were always more,' mean to you?

Always
Marianne Lyon

You were always brighter than
pale finger of light
streaming though my window

Warming laughter crooned
soft notes   pulling
stretching endless

Eyes   liquid amber lifted
carried me into
sweet childhood adventures

You arrive in my memory
drift like breeze-born leaf
outstretched fingers

pull me up from stumbling fall
like blow-ball of a dandelion
I fly into your arms

In dim recesses of my aging mind
You were always more
and as I watch sky's edge

rosy sunset   rework feelings
not entirely welcome
You were always courageous

Desperate decision
huge as a cliff
towers before me

No more tomorrows   no more excuses
disappointments weary themselves out
Last chance leaps up through

crust of my mind
Like brave crocus in early spring.
I begin to let my sprout grow

Invite setting sun leap onto me in
extravagant tumble
You were always more

I'm always not far away*
Marianne Lyon

Autumn sun morning

Bridge radiates

Comfortable bench   holds her slumping

Depression amplifies

Enhances

Fading dreams

Exiting life   a possibility

Her heart flattened by misery

Inner grey skies

Jump off bridge   a possibility

Knowing   feeling connections   impossible

Lifetime maybe over   when a

Man   dark haired stranger arrives

Next to her he sits   shady

Or a pervert

Portion of you I am   from your future

Queries abound   her eyes widen   mouth ajar

Ray of hope he sends

Sadness exhales above her ocean of grief

Thomas is my name   never far away

Understand   she wants to believe his bidding to

Value life's preciousness now

Wondering   tears well up

Xenagogue tells her of sacred connections

Your heart desires to attach to divine

Zany moments will come in handy too   he grins

*A found poem from *Abigail's Unexpected Connection* by Geoffrey K.

Leigh

Abigail's Unexpected Connection
Geoffrey K. Leigh

Late morning sun radiates off autumn red bridge that emerges out of the grassy knoll by the bay. Rather than basking in the sun's warmth, Abigail swamps in the all too familiar grayness and intestinal knots that permeate her abdomen, further nurturing her ever-present self-loathing.

She slumps atop the bench of a silver metal table resting comfortably on a cement slab encircled by grass. She gazes at the sail boats working their way towards shore. Abigail notices sunlight that embraces the salted water and creates a glow that is unmatched by the kiss of even the world's greatest lovers.

At least that's what she supposes, not knowing any herself. She certainly doesn't fit such a picture. That thought lowers her further into the grayness and knots.

Today, Abigail's heart is flattened by life's misery, two dimensional black and white, even amongst all this beauty. Her tumultuous divorce and the resulting financial drain left few resources, culminating in her decrepit studio apartment. The fading of her dream and increasing debt from the steep alimony only provide additional sustenance to the inner gray skies.

In an attempt to change her mood on this day off, she thought maybe a bus ride and walk to the Welcome Center would be a good exercise and enhance her outlook. She donned a bright yellow blouse, a nice contrast to her dark hair and eyes, blue jeans and loafers. She wants to feel comfortable with whatever she chooses.

Yet, Abigail still isn't sure whether to walk down along the marina or take a leap off the bridge. Go right or left? Her options garner equal appeal in her present state.

Abigail desires to focus on the providence to live in such a beautiful city, a coveted location since her childhood in the Phoenix desert. Now she is here, through luck and hard work. Yet, she experiences joy as fleeting.

She wants to appreciate her current existence. When the dark pit opens up, it sucks in all the light, joy, and possibilities of an exciting life, despite her recently successful novel. No public reading seems triumphant enough, no amount of sales sufficient to overcome the heavy weight pulling on her heart.

"Do you mind if I sit here?" asks the stranger standing on the far side of the table, a man she hadn't noticed approach. "It seems to be the best view of this lovely bridge, and the kids at those other tables seem to be a bit it rowdy."

Abigail's body recoils as she turns to see a young dark haired man dressed in preppy tan slacks and white shirt with a short straight collar. Her response remains sluggish, like her thoughts and any desire.

"Ah .. yeah, . . . I . . . I . . . I guess that's fine. But I don't feel like talking."

"That's OK. I don't mean to disturb you. I just want to take in the view."

This man looks oddly familiar. But Abigail can't recall where she might have encountered him.

The two strangers sit at the table. She focuses on the sparkling water, trying to internalize the beauty. He stares at the expanse of metal crossing the mouth to the huge ocean.

"Sorry, but I am just so taken by how they build magnificent structures over such large bodies of water."

"Yeah, it's impressive," responds Abigail, her voice flat and falling as she ends her remark. She considers leaving. Again not sure which direction to take, she remains seated.

"Do you live in the city?" the stranger inquires.

Abigail's dark eyes look into the stranger, unsure whether to respond.

"Yeah, about 8 years now."

"Wow, lucky," the stranger responds. After a modicum of silence, he continues. "I hear people jump off that bridge from time to time, most of them not surviving. That true?"

Abigail leans back when she hears the question with a churning in her stomach. She guesses the word gets around, even to people not from the area.

"Yeah, sometimes. Almost none of them survive, which is why they are building a barrier to prevent such attempts."

"I guess if you're really wanting to go, that would be a better way than most."

Abigail again considers whether to respond. The stranger seems nice enough. But rather pushy. She still wants to avoid casual conversation, which only interferes with her decision of which direction to proceed. That irritates her further.

"I guess it wouldn't be as bad as some or as messy as others," responds Abigail, hoping her comment will finalize the conversation.

"I know you said you didn't feel like talking right now, but I was wondering if you would indulge me in a short conversation. And if you say no, that's fine too," says the stranger.

"About what? I'm not in the best space to chat."

"Yes, I get that. But it's kind of important to do now, I think."

"Important how? Do you know me or something?"

"Yeah, kind of. And I've been seeking you out for a while."

"How do you know me? You some kind of detective?"

"I guess you could call me that, but not in a traditional sense."

Abigail's face turns red, as her stomach churning amplifies. He seems to know something about her but continues his evasive responses. She starts to wonder just what he wants and gets suspicious that this guy might be shady or some kind of pervert.

"So what do you want? What's your name?"

"My name is Thomas. I want to talk to you about the decision you currently are facing. I want to talk it through with you before you do something that will impact you for a long time."

"What are you talking about? What decision? What do you know about me? What do you want from me?" Abigail's agitation increases with the vagueness of Thomas' responses.

"OK, this is not going to be easy for you to digest. But I sense that I'm agitating you. And that won't help our discussion. So I'll just spell it out the best way I can."

"You a cop? Internal Revenue? Who the hell are you, mister?"

"I'm you from the future. Or rather, I'm a future portion of you."

Abigail looks at him for a few seconds, then she bursts into laughter.

"Well, OK, I didn't see that one coming. That's good. You need a few bucks or something? I don't have much, but how could I not give to myself from the future? That's a new one for me!"

Abigail continues to look at this guy. He lacks any hint of a smile. But already, she's spinning ideas for a new novel. The beauty of this place hasn't lightened her mood, but this comical story seems to be helping.

"You have a great presentation! Almost believable," she continues.

Thomas looks at Abigail intently without responding to her ridicule. He finally smiles.

"I told you this wasn't going to be easy for you."

"Seriously, what do you want from me?" Abigail reaches into her purse and pulls out her wallet, finds a couple of dollar bills and hands them to the man. "OK, we square? You'll leave me alone now?"

Thomas pushes the money away.

"I'm not interested in your money. I'm more concerned about your consideration of suicide."

Abigail rests her arm on the table, her palm still weighing down the money, as she stares at this stranger. She now is oblivious to the table or salt air. Her eyes have widened, her mouth ajar. She looks deeply into Thomas' eyes, wondering how he has any idea of what she's been contemplating.

"Well, that was a good guess, mister, finding me alone here at the bridge. But you're wrong. I'm just out for a walk, heading down to the marina next."

"It seems you haven't made a final decision. And the marina is your other option, which is a much better one from my perspective. If you were to end up deciding on the first option, that would impact us for lifetimes. And that is what I want to discuss."

"You know, this was cute for a few minutes, but I am getting tired of this game."

"Oh, Abigail, this is a kind of game. But how you play has long term impacts. And I have traced the impacts back to you and your current decision. I'm hoping you'll choose a different option."

"I still don't have any idea what you are talking about."

"OK, let me lay it out more clearly. I am much of you seven lifetimes from now. As I was getting in touch with past lives, I came back to this point in time when you jumped off this bridge and died. While I understand your desire to give up, I also saw how the next three lifetimes were spent basically learning to place a higher value on life and consciousness through various challenges."

Abigail looks into the man's dark eyes. Something tells her the man is being earnest. Yet this is too weird to be believable. She swallows, takes a deep breath as he continues.

"The first one after this we lived in a small village that was ravaged by war and starvation. The next one was nicer in that we had lots of money and were weighing the relationship between having riches and a more conscious life. In the third lifetime, we were monks who were faced with following orders to take advantage of people's finances or really help them develop greater consciousness."

Abigail huffs out her breath. She looks around, unable to decide where to exit. She wants to leave. This whole interaction appears absurd.

"Then I also looked at what might happen if we decided not to kill ourself today. You can learn to value life's precious experience to become more conscious now or later. But we wouldn't have to retrace such issues if you make a different decision in this life."

Abigail's hands begin to shake as she diverts her eyes to the boats again.

"Ah, this is nice and all. But I can't breathe. I think I need some fresh air. I'm going to walk down to the marina."

"Abigail, you're sitting outdoors on a hill with fresh air all around you!"

"Well, I need to go for a walk."

"Give me five minutes. If I can't convince you to reconsider your decision, I'll walk you onto the bridge myself. You're always at choice. Fair enough?"

"Alrigh, five minutes. Go."

"When you were a young girl, living in Phoenix, all you could think about was living by the Pacific Ocean and becoming a writer. You moved here and finished your first novel, which was moderately successful. Your publisher wanted you to do another. Then the depression set in, followed by a divorce and financial strain. Even in your novel, you were suggesting the importance of being more conscious."

"Yea, OK, you know a little bit about me. So what?"

"Consciousness has always been a priority with you. You learned to meditate, you read a lot about expanding your energy and vision. You go to energy and consciousness workshops. And one big disappointment in your marriage was the lack of priority Susan had in exploring consciousness."

"Everyone knows that about Susan. Tell me something everyone doesn't know."

"Your heart aches to be connected to what you perceive as the Divine. And that is part of your desire to end your life right now. You hope that you can feel in death what eludes you currently in this life."

Abigail could feel the tears welling up in her eyes, then begin to trickle down her cheeks. She didn't even attempt to hide them. Her hands felt sweaty, her breathing shallow. Her chest begins to ache. But she couldn't deny what this stranger just described as the secret of her heart.

"So what do I do? Or rather, what do we do? What is the other option that you are suggesting?"

Thomas now had her full attention. He felt Abigail's heart melt a bit and create a small crack somewhere in its energetic field.

"I recommend that we take advantage of this current opportunity to work harder to create such a connection in this life. Expand into consciousness now rather than put it off for other lifetimes. Nourish the part of you that still lives. I know you're hurting, and it feels like any connection is impossible in this life. But it's always possible. What's important is that we keep trying. And I will help all I can in this exploration."

"But if you are me, then how about you just doing it? You seem to know more and have greater confidence in this possibility."

Thomas broke into a heart filled smile.

"You see, we're much greater than what you appear to be here or the way you define yourself. We are in this together. But we each only control part of our collective consciousness. Your part of our conscious being remains in charge of this lifetime. I can't control your part. That would be taking away the choice this lifetime gives you and the learning you contribute to the whole. I can only help you see a larger vision. Then you get to choose what to do. But I can be a support in your process, just like Tim and Vanessa and other friends are. In the end, none of us can make the choice for you. That is the gift and curse of this journey. Unless, of course, we give away our freedom to choose as well."

"Yeah, my friends are a nice support. But they can't remove the pain, my heart drowning in sadness and grief."

"No, and I can't either. But I can assist you in elevating your gratitude for life and beauty, allowing your heart to breathe above that ocean of sadness and grief. For both depression and gratitude can be parts of this life. Choice is allowing us to see beyond the gloom without ignoring either the darkness or the light as a part of living. And I will help in that cosmic connection. That's something where I have experience. But rather than taking three lifetimes to learn from the choice you face today, I suggest you explore and choose that connection in this lifetime, allowing us a deeper exploration over the next six. That is what I am recommending we do. I can't do it without your part of us."

Abigail takes a slow, deep breath. As she exhales, she notices her body relax into the metal seat. Her hands rest on the table. Into Thomas's eyes, she looks deeper.

For the first time in weeks, Abigail feels a ray of hope in her chest. Her breathing slows and deepens.

She wants to believe what this "stranger" is saying. But it all sounds so weird. So far outside her realm of possibility. Yet, she notices a sanguine spark in his heart. She hopes such a light might shine on her own divine connection and transform her current wretched experience.

"Alright, I'll commit to trying this option for a week and see how it goes."

"Two years."

"What? No, no, a month."

"Eighteen months."

"Six months."

"A year."

"OK. But if at the end of that time I'm not feeling any better, I get to jump off that bridge with your help."

"Deal. And if you are feeling better and experiencing a closer connection to the Divine, more gratitude for life and all you have, you will use your entire life to seek greater consciousness in whatever way feels most appropriate to you."

"Ah . . . well . . . OK, I guess. Deal. Now, how about we get some lunch."

"Before you do that, I would like to give you one suggestion that may assist you in this exploration."

"OK. That would be nice."

"How would you feel about a brief meditation? Right here, right now?"

"Ah . . . I guess so."

"Great. Close your eyes and slowly take a deep breath."

Abigail looks at the people around her, all in a world of their own. Her eyelids close. Thomas continues tenderly.

"Focus your attention on your breath as you inhale . . . then exhale."

Thomas pauses, letting Abigail's attention remain with her breath.

"Now another, slow inhale . . . and exhale."

Another short pause.

"This time, as you inhale, let your attention move to your heart. Allow the energy and even your heart itself to expand. Just a little bit each time . . . It's alright if it contracts a bit with the exhale. But let the energy in and around the heart enlarge, as if you were intentionally creating a heart expansion. If you experience it as more open too, so much the better."

Abigail continues to focus on her heart. The noise from children running, people chatting, and the breeze on the hill diminishes. Slowly, all sounds cascade into the depths of silence as she returns her attention to her heart. With each breath, her heart eases more, expands a little.

"Take one more slow deep breath, inviting your heart to energetically open further. As you sit in this space, ask this question: 'Is there a connection to some divine source with which I can link?' Then just wait to see what happens. What's the response of the universe to your request? It doesn't have to be exactly those words. But follow that intention."

Abigail asks the question in her mind, then waits for what happens. What she notices is a sense of serenity permeating her heart. She opens her eyes and looks at Thomas.

"I didn't hear an answer. Do I just keep doing it?"

"Yes. Keep asking the question and being accessible. Sometimes it happens quickly. In other cases, it takes time. But it will occur at a very subtle level. So be sure to pay close attention. That's the place of such responses. That's the place of sacred communication. The trick is that these connections are not far away. They never leave us. We simply turn our focus elsewhere. Desire them, allow them, and pay attention for when we show up and hear them."

"Is that it? Is that all I have to do?"

"Not necessarily. But it's a place to start. Then other intuitive ideas may appear. Just stay open and pay attention at a very subtle level."

"OK . . . thanks. Now do you want to get some lunch? I'm hungry."

"Well, I'm happy to go with you, but I can't really eat. I'm here to some extent physically, but not totally. Not like you. It's like I can make it just enough for you to see and talk with me. But I don't get to enjoy the physical sensations that you do in this life or I do in my lifetime."

"So you couldn't have sex here?" chuckles Abigail, partly to break the intensity, as she often does.

"Oh, you had to go there, didn't you!" laughs Thomas. "Go ahead, rub it in."

"Well, I guess I can't. You wouldn't feel that either!" responds Abigail as he begins to laugh out loud.

"Glad you keep your sense of humor. That will come in handy too. I had better go now. This is exhausting. You have a good lunch, and I'll be around. Thanks for taking the time to talk today and your willingness to probe an alternative choice. And I promise to support you in whatever way feels most useful to you. Just call on me when you want support."

Thomas reaches out and places his hand on top of Abigail's.

"I'm always not far away. Especially under the circumstances. And now I know how to connect with you more easily."

Abigail looks into Thomas's eyes.

"Thank you."

She gets up and heads towards the marina to find some lunch.

While the depression has not lifted, her heart feels lighter. As she walks away, the words echo in her head.

I'm always not far away.

Writing Prompts 7

1. Do you have an exploration in your life? How would you describe it? Take a few moments to write about it in prose or poetry form.

2. What does "the connection" mean to you? Describe what comes to mind and how you would tell others about it?

3. Imagine, then write a verse or short story about an invisible person who picks up a pen and starts writing to you.

4. Tune in to a station you don't normally listen to and write a poem inspired by the first song or message you hear.

5. Imagine you are from another planet, stuck on earth and longing for home. What would you express in such a situation?

CHAPTER EIGHT

Exploration

As you read the pieces in this chapter, consider the following:

What imagined setting or issue might inspire you to write?

Truth*
Marianne Lyon

Explore everything
reach everywhere
this moment
past lives
remember reminders
imagine imagining
befriend memories
cuddle   play with fantasies
wander   wonder
live
don't squash
naggings
unsettlings
detect them   feel them
sculpt them   love them
allow
inspect
discover   similarities
protect   connections
scour   details
welcome unexpected
respond with joy
believe
truthfully live
truthfully abide
now
repeat after me
"All the truth   all the time"

*A found poem from *The Living Truth Detector* by Geoffrey K. Leigh

Carrying Grandpa*
Marianne Lyon

Somewhere deep in my belly
I remember statue-self standing
in grandparents' kitchen
sunlight erases room of shadows
watch grandpa toot wooden flute
an etched pipe he carried in his rucksack
on ship to Ellis Island*

nimble fingers   marching soldiers
ruddy cheeks puff
like billows of dad's accordion
melodies swim out
slow tunes drift
like lazy duck on a pond
then race into ruckus melodies
eyebrows arch   fingers dance

I begin to pop with flutes feral falsetto
follow wild pied-piper
no matter where we march
the light follows us around
tables   stools   ironing board
from wooden nostrils
another tune breathes out
something beckons me
to stand in its breath
I settle   flushed cheeks
bathed clean in familiar

the stream of him
flowed into me that afternoon
his flute nourished
refrains spun a ball of yarn
that knitted my life
like waves spreading onto the shore
seeping into sand
we became one
when I look deep into grandpa
I find myself

*Born in Bribir Croatia
Sailed from Liverpool on the Ship: Cedric, 1906

The Living Truth Detector[1]
Geoffrey K. Leigh

Almost five adventurous years passed since Pablo's birth to Emilio and Sara, an intended conception with unexpected consequences. The birth occurred normally for mother and child.

All systems in little Pablo's body appeared to be operating well as far as medical professionals could discern. But apparently, the scientific community lacks tests for some human functions. Nor do most scientists recognize they exist. Emilio and Sara, however, experienced the results of just such a mysterious and perfectly functioning system.

Sara and Emilio met in college while she studied medicine and he explored painting and sculpting. They fell madly in love and married after Sara's residency.

As both grew up in the Bay Area, they decided to remain near family. They eventually settled in Napa, allowing Sara to join a cardiology practice and Emilio to teach part-time at the community college while continuing his creative endeavors.

When the new parents found out Sara was pregnant, they responded with joy at the prospect of starting their family. They wanted to continue their careers while also spending as much time as possible with their new baby.

Sara stayed home half-time for two months after Pablo's birth, then Emilio took the lead caring for their son when Sara returned to work full-time.

After the first year, they hired a young woman who immigrated from Panama to care for their son. They could focus more time on their careers

---

1. Originally published in *Mertiage: Collected Works from Napa Valley Writers*, 2019. Gnarly Vine Press, Napa, CA.

and provide consistent care for Pablo. In addition, their son could learn to speak Spanish more fluently.

During the first three years, Pablo developed along a pretty typical path. He smiled and laughed a lot, exploring everything within his reach.

As he developed, he started spending time with his dad in Emilio's studio. His father created a work space shortly after Pablo's second birthday by separating off the third-car portion of the garage. He installed a room air conditioner, and an additional north window to improve the light for painting.

Following Pablo's fourth birthday, he and Isabel, the care-taker, increasingly explored Emilio's trove of art supplies and materials.

"Ah, Emilio, maybe you come see the bowl Pablo make," said Isabel, her voice shaky.

Emilio put down his brush and walked over to the wheel where Pablo and Isabel were working.

"Did you make that, Isabel?" Emilio inquired.

"I turn the wheel, but Pablo make the bowl!"

Emilio heard the words, but he had a hard time believing them.

"Really? You didn't help him?"

"No, Pablo make the bowl."

Emilio continued to stare at the nearly perfect bowl Pablo had crafted.

"Wow, Pablo, that's terrific! I'm amazed at how quickly you've learned to make pottery!"

"Because I used to make these when my family lived by the water. But we had to kick the wheel."

Emilio and Isabel looked at each other, mouths gaping open. Neither knew what to say. They turned back to stare once again at the bowl.

"Well... I guess you kind of remembered," stammered Emilio.

He looked imploringly at Isabel. She remained at a loss for words.

"Nice work, Pablo," says his dad.

Not quite knowing what else to do, Emilio went back to his easel. He sits in front of his work while his mind wanders the rest of the afternoon.

When Sara got home, Emilio told her about the experience he had with their son.

"He said what?" quizzed Sara.

"He said he used to make these things when his family lived by the water."

"Oh, he is just sharing one of his imaginary stories. I think you're over-reacting, Emilio. You can't take a four-year-old that literally. Their brains are developing and they are still learning," explained Sara, exhaling a sigh. "It's nothing serious."

"You think so? You think he's just being creative? He sounded so decisive when he said it," continued Emilio.

"Come on, honey. There's no other way to explain it."

"OK. You know more about this than me. But still, there was conviction in his voice that sounded quite unusual. It was really odd and surprising."

"That is how kids relate to fantasy. They can sound very sure of them-selves, even when it isn't true," replied Sara, apparently wanting to put the issue to rest.

Emilio let the discussion die. Yet, it didn't feel finished to him.

He began to read about children who reported past-life experiences. How some of the information they shared was verifiable and accurate.

Several days later, Emilio decided to ask Pablo a few more questions regarding his story of another life.

"I've been wondering about your experience by the water. Can you tell me anything else that you remember about the place?" he asked in a matter-of-fact tone. Or at least with as much casualness as he could muster under the circumstances.

"*Sí,* I remember a few things. I had some brothers and shared a room with two of them. My father went fishing, and we ate lots of fish and fresh fruits. We wore looser clothing. And there was a big building at the edge of the water where it was fun to explore and play games." Pablo responded again in a matter-of-fact manner and exhibited the same confidence he had earlier.

"Do you remember the name of the town where you lived?" inquired Emilio, increasingly curious about this whole affair.

"*un poco*, but not really. It was like Sada, something like that," Pablo replied. Then he went back to a drawing he was making.

The next morning as Sara and Emilio were having coffee on the patio, Emilio shared his interactions with Pablo.

"I think he really does remember some of these things, much like in this book I've been reading about children reporting past-life experiences. I think it would be interesting to investigate this further," said Emilio with some excitement, as if he had discovered a new painting technique he wanted to pursue.

"Let's not get too excited about this," chuckled Sara. "Pablo has a terrific imagination, which is wonderful. I don't want to squash it. But I also don't want to reinforce such tales and encourage them any further. It will only make it more difficult for him to make friends and relate to teachers later on. People will think he's strange."

"Ok. But I still think there is something to this," responded Emilio, as a final parry just before losing the fencing match.

Emilio and Sara said nothing more about the incident. Nor did they ask Pablo anything further about his reported memory.

Still, Emilio kept reading about children who made such reports and wondered about the possibility of Pablo's story being accurate. He kept looking at old castles in Europe that might be near water, but none came close to what Pablo had described.

Eventually, he got caught up in a new piece of art he wanted to finish, and that refocused his attention and energy.

Nearly six months later, on a chilly Saturday morning, Sara and Pablo were eating breakfast at the kitchen island. Sara was enjoying a slow morning and wanted to get several things done around the house. But she was in no hurry to get started. Her coffee was still hot, and she held the cup with both hands to warm them a bit as she breathed in the aroma.

"Could we go play in the park today, Mommy?" inquired Pablo.

"No, Pablo, I don't have any time for that today. Maybe another day soon."

"That doesn't feel like the truth," responded Pablo.

"What do you mean by that?" asked Sara indignantly.

"I see this cloud come over your chest. And I feel it in *my* chest. It feels like you're hiding something. I remember that cloud like I remember living by the water," answered Pablo.

"Well, I'm not. You're simply mistaken," replied Sara rather sternly.

"Ok," said Pablo as he slid off his stool and headed for the studio.

Sara's stomach tightened. She felt tension in her throat. This sudden encounter with her young son stunned her. She reflected on the many things she wanted to get done that day. She had told the truth.

And what right did Pablo have to question me, his mother? she thought.

She continued to sip her coffee and feel the correctness of her statement. Yet something nagged at her, something unsettled.

It only took three more sips of coffee to turn on the lights: she *did* have time to go to the park, but she also had other plans and things she would rather do.

So we are both right, thought Sara.

But that unsettled feeling crept in again.

No, he's right. I wasn't really truthful. I wanted to do something else, but I didn't want to explain myself. I didn't want to have to justify doing what I wanted to do rather than go play in the park.

While the story of living by the water was surprising, knowing when someone was not telling the truth was even more unnerving and shocking. She had no idea *anyone* could do that, especially a boy not yet five-years-old.

Sara finished her coffee and turned to her tasks for the day, feeling the sudden urgency to get things done.

As the day went on, she felt more settled regarding the way things had gone with Pablo.

Besides, she thought, *he probably doesn't really know, or will remember, what went on between us this morning. He's just a child, after all.*

A few days later, the two boys were in the studio. Emilio worked on his canvas and Pablo continued his sketch with black ink and paper, like his father had shown him.

After some time, Emilio rose to stretch and take a break. He wandered over to see how Pablo was doing. He stopped and stared at his son's drawing.

There, on the paper, was a drawing of an old castle surrounded by a body of water. Emilio focused more intently on the drawing. He was sure he had seen something like that before, but he couldn't remember where. It looked a bit Roman, maybe with a Middle Eastern twist, though he wasn't sure why.

"Very nice, young man. Where did you see that picture?" asked Emilio.

"I saw it when I lived near the water. It's like the building we had by our village."

"Son, that's very well done!"

"*Gracias*," responded Pablo.

Emilio racked his memory. There remained a similarity with some image he had seen. But he was unable to connect it with an artist.

He walked over to his computer. He sat down and scoured the Internet for some clues.

Emilio started looking through pictures of castles in the UK, France, Spain, and other parts of the Mediterranean. Finally, he came across a well-known Scottish artist, David Roberts, who made many drawings of places and people in the Middle East.

As Emilio was going through Roberts's work, he stopped suddenly and stared at a picture entitled "Citadel of Sidon." There, from a different angle and more elaborately rendered, was a castle very similar to what Pablo had drawn. Emilio looked further and found another Roberts drawing of Sidon. This one had a view similar to Pablo's drawing but at a greater distance from the Citadel. Still, the similarity was uncanny.

Emilio asked Pablo to come look at his computer. Pablo put down his pen and walked over, then looked at the drawing by Roberts.

"*Bonito, Padre.* That artist must have lived in the same town as me."

Pablo headed back towards the table where he was working.

"Wait, Pablo—come back for a minute, *por favor.*"

Pablo walked back over and looked up at his dad.

"Have you ever seen this picture before?" inquired Emilio.

Pablo looked intently at the computer screen, then turned back to his dad.

"*No, Padre.* But it's very nice," replied his son.

Emilio went back to the first drawing he had found and asked the same question.

"Nope, not that one either. But I like this one more. It's a better drawing of the building."

"OK, thanks, son. You can go back to your work now."

Emilio didn't know what to think. Had his son seen the drawings somewhere? Did he just copy what he saw? But how would he remember so much detail? Emilio was familiar with Roberts's work from art school. He was sure he didn't have any copies of this drawings around the studio or house.

Emilio walked back over to Pablo's work table to look at the drawing again.

"How's it coming along? You about finished?" he asked.

"Almost. I'll finish today."

"May I take it when you're finished? I would love to put it in a frame and hang it in the hallway next to the painting of the old Paris street I did last year. Would that be all right with you?"

"*Si, Padre.* I'd like that."

Later, Emilio went back to his computer and printed out the two drawings by Roberts. After Pablo finished his piece, he took the Roberts' drawings, along with Pablo's work, to show Sara.

"This is the drawing of the castle in the village by the sea that Pablo mentioned last year where he learned to throw pots. He finished it today. Then I showed him these two drawings by David Roberts. They're of the Citadel of Sidon, which, in Arabic, is pronounced Sayda. Roberts made them in the 1800s."

Sara studied Pablo's drawing, then looked closely at both prints by Roberts.

"Do you think he saw these prints somewhere before?"

"I asked him that, and he said no. I don't see how he could have, either. I know about them from a class in college. But I don't think I have any copies of them here," responded Emilio. His eyes widened, his cheeks flushed of red, and his voice rose.

"I don't know what to think," stammered Sara.

As Pablo came in from the studio, Sara looked at him, half smiling.

"Great drawing, honey! Now I believe what you said about having lived by the water before."

"That doesn't feel true, *Mami*."

Sara took her last sip of tea while reflecting on what she just said.

"You're right, Pablo. I *want* to believe what you said about living by the water before. It's difficult to believe that children remember such things as past lives. But I promise to work on it, because I love you and I'm clear that you tell the truth. Knowing that you can tell when someone else is not speaking the truth may be an even bigger challenge for me."

Emilio leaned over and gave Sara a sideways hug.

"It isn't easy for me either," he said to Pablo. "And I appreciate the information you gave us to help with this shift. I had no idea children could do this."

Then Emilio turned to Sara and looked into her eyes.

"Do you remember a basic request you made when we got married? You requested 'All the truth, all the time.' I guess we got a reminder of incorporating that more pervasively in our lives!" chuckled Emilio.

Pablo walked over to them.

"*That* feels like the truth, *Mami y Padre*," he said with a smile.

Writing Prompts 8

1. What imagined setting or issue might inspire a poem or short story you have not previously envisioned? Try writing about something magical, yet seemingly impossible that interests you.

2. Befriend a memory and write a letter to her.

3. Is there an unsettled nagging that you need or want to explore?

4. Write a short poem inspired by the phrase, "the stream of him or her flowed into me."

5. Reread The Living Truth Detector and write your own found poem (as defined in Writing Prompt #1).

6. Reread Carrying Grandpa and write a short story based on the ideas from the poem.

CHAPTER NINE

Divergent Roads

As you read the poems and short story in this chapter, consider the following:

Think about a time in your life when you couldn't make an important decision.

Wannabe*
Marianne Lyon

Bright paper pad stares
my eyes glaze over   search
for inspiration

I peer out window
hope perspective will generate
new ideas

Heart   not in writing
It's still at the winery
dream of making wine

Harvesting ripe grapes
crushing   tasting from barrel
back with grandfather

Blank paper calls me
preferred alternative ferments
pushed to the sidelines

"I want to change jobs"
from first sip to final swallow
taste fragrant vintage

Make wines that bring joy
to people's interactions
Happiness not fears

Do not want to live
other people's dreams
they said were my dreams

My wife   son take leave
I fall into darkened funk
yet my dream is strong

Slowly   funk releases
joy returns to my life
Write letters to my son

Hear grandfather's song
Winter prepares for Springtime
Regeneration

*A found poem from *The Wannabe* by Geoffrey K. Leigh

The Wannabe
Geoffrey K. Leigh

The bright paper pad stares back at him as his dark eyes glaze over, daring him to defile the surface with nonsensical words. He searched for any type of inspiration he might discover from the sun's reflective glare.

On one side of Luca's pad lies piles of notes from his research results. On the other side remain stacks of books and journals used for the literature review.

The methods section emerged straightforward and about as dull as his wit at the moment. He stuffed the results section with key findings and a meager attempt to highlight something that might seduce interest from the journal editor and reviewers.

But the implications? Three times he has written, 'who cares.' He begrudgingly crossed out the phrase after agreeing with it each time.

Then he thought of his broad shouldered, dark haired grandfather and his unspoken concern for each vine in his vineyard. He hummed as he worked to encourage their maturation.

Now, Luca needs to care. To nurture this article into fresh significance. Attempt to blossom some ideas that will bear academic fruit.

While he's not yet a heavily published researcher, it doesn't take much expertise to know that such lack of caring will not get this article into print. Implications? If he sits here much longer, frozen in space on this mildly comfortable black chair, the dean soon could write that old academic saying on his office door. 'He published and perished anyway.'

He glances around his office for any possible stimulus. One thing to generate some useful idea in his head that could find its way into the document.

He notices the creative quote typed on the otherwise blank piece of paper haphazardly hung on the pinboard above his computer. *Writing is easy. All you have to do is stare at a blank piece of paper until blood seeps from your forehead, forced out by a fabulous new idea.*

He can't remember who shared this sage wisdom. Some economics professor somewhere in some university. He wishes he had this author's phone number. He might call for any additional writing hints and brilliant suggestions.

Luca rises to peer out his third floor window, thinking a larger perspective might help generate new ideas for this final section. His work thus far today has been to no avail other than spawning more internal pressure.

He notices the sun bleached sand being refreshed by ocean waves. He watches strollers on the beach. He envies the couple sitting on a towel under shade at a tree clump's edge. Yet, he prefers to be on that cruise ship sailing off into the distance.

Again, his grandfather's image arises amidst his frustration. His olive skin. A frequent smile amid smooth face lines.

Luca's irritation softens as he recalls his granddad focusing his attention on careful pruning of the vines, cleaning of the barrels, and blending of his wine. Yet, he never seemed irritated as Luca feels now. His granddad patiently worked on every aspect in detail. His unspoken concern focused on completing each task with precision.

The real implications are that if this article is sufficiently strong, it has a chance to be included in the upcoming special issue on promising biochemistry research. Such a publication in a prestigious journal would strengthen Luca's chances for tenure, essential for his relationship with Elena, his wife.

She agreed to leave her family on the east coast three years ago for this enviable opportunity at a respected medical research university in southern California. He committed to do all he could to make this position successful.

Yet the inner pressure reaffirms his concern. His heart isn't in this piece. It remains at the winery he and Elena visited last month during their trip to Napa. He frequently considers how he might make a better wine than they experienced at their last tasting, their seventh winery visit over the three-day-journey. This would be only his second article of the academic year.

Realizing a larger view only takes him further away from his writing, he sits back down to the paper with scratched marks on the upper third. His lean body elevates in the chair when his phone rings.

"How's it going, dear? You asked me to check in, and this is your 'wake up call'" says Elena. "I got everything unpacked from our trip. Then I realized I needed more cereal and juice. But Angelo went down early, and we'll need it tomorrow. Could you pick some up on your way home?"

"Of course. I'll stop at the store just down the street."

"And how is the article coming along? Will you have the final product submitted by Friday's deadline?" she asks.

Luca's hands get sweatier and his nausea increases.

"It's coming together. Slower than I want, yet I'm making some headway. It's going to take additional time, I'm afraid. But I think I'll be fine," he says, hoping his verbalization of intention will encourage the outcome. "I'm probably going to have to work late."

"Well, don't forget to stop on your way home."

"Yeah, I'll be sure to pick them up. Thanks for checking in."

Luca hangs up as he looks back at his writing paper. He cares a lot about his research, hoping to extend the work he started with his dissertation. He considers whether another cup of coffee from the lounge will help, then looks down to see his mug still half full.

He takes a gulp, spits it back into the cup, then walks it down the hall to the microwave. The clicking of the appliance reminds him of his deadline countdown, and it's coming fast. The bell dings. Coffee ready. He not.

He gets his cup, takes a sip as he trudges back to the office, then sets it over the desk stain. He picks up his phone and calls his lab manager.

"What were those two implications we were talking about the other day? I forgot to write them down."

His assistant reminds him, and Luca thanks him as he replaces the handset.

He's back at this paper, writing down the suggested implications, remembering it's easier to edit than write from a blank mind.

As his left hemisphere directs the writing, his heart diverts his attention. He keeps getting a picture of him harvesting grapes, crushing them, then tasting from the barrel as they did at their second winery.

He enjoyed his summer work as an adolescent at his grandfather's vineyards in the Central Valley. But medical research jobs pay much more. And this department bought him, lock, stock, and research pedigree.

Even consideration of a change in positions feels like a betrayal to his major professor, his father, who was a leading thoracic surgeon at NYU, and his wife. He isn't in touch with his former professor, and his father passed two years ago. But how could he explain this to Elena? She agreed to move across the country because of this outstanding academic opportunity.

The half blank paper calls him back to other implications. He continues to work on his article while his preferred options ferment on the sidelines.

As he sets the alternative dream aside, Luca realizes he now can discuss the relevance of his project. He writes out the two ideas from the lab manager's comments, then makes bullet points for two other significant inferences that would please his father. They directly relate to a biochemical idea the two of them talked about from one of his father's biggest surgical cases.

Finally, his left hemisphere switches into high gear. Luca's pencil is flying, trying to keep up with his thoughts, which seem to make his spelling deteriorate rapidly. Yet he would rather be frustrated at creating unreadable words than having no damn idea what to say.

After three more hours of implication dredging, followed by some editing, Luca is satisfied with his rough draft. He tears off his papers and puts them in the tray for his secretary to type. He has another day for final editing. He'll have his lab manager read the entire article after reviewing it once more.

Feeling close enough to quit, his heart questions swirl up for direct consideration. He grabs his satchel, locks his door, walks toward his car.

One shopping stop before home.

"Hey, Elena, here are the cereal and juices you wanted," Luca announces as he enters his front door with bag in hand.

"Wow, you're home earlier than expected."

"I'm not interrupting an affair or anything, am I?" says Luca, wanting to lighten the mood.

Elena laughs. "Not with this wild child back awake. Thanks for picking these up. Did you get some dinner? Ready for a glass of wine?"

"Yes, I grabbed some food on campus. Wine would be great."

"If you'll get Angelo back down, I'll open a bottle."

"I'm on it."

Luca picks up his son and takes the milk bottle Elena hands him. He hums a favorite version of *Hushabye* as he rocks his nine-month-old treasure. He walks slowly toward the baby's crib, staring deeply into his son's eyes, enjoying this moment with him.

He knows Angelo would also be very young if he were a new red Cab, developing in a barrel. Luca chuckles at this absurd comparison. Yet it brings together two loves in his life; his family and great tasting wines.

As Luca returns to the kitchen, Elena hands him a glass of Stags Leap Cab to celebrate the completion of the research article draft. It's only six years since the 1976 "Judgment of Paris," when this unknown winery beat the French Cabs and shocked the world. While this vintage is two years later than the one in competition, it still is tasting delicious and complex from first sip to final swallow.

This is what Luca longs to do. After the trip to Napa, it has become clear that this is his heart's dream.

"Congratulations on completing your draft. This publication will be great for your tenure review in three years," says Elena as she leans back against the soft couch and raises her glass to her scholarly husband.

"Dear One, I want to change jobs."

The words rush out with such a heavy flow of desire, Luca can't stop them. He intended to be more subtle about his intention, paving the way with a hint or two at least. The internal struggle and pressure to generate academic excellence produced a stronger flow than he anticipated.

"You want to WHAT?" responds his wife as she carefully puts her glass down on the side table with her trembling hand.

"I can't continue long term . . . . . not in this kind of position. This was my dad's dream . . . . . not really mine."

Luca takes a breath, despite the tightness he notices in his chest.

"I thought I would be happy in it . . . . . in part . . . . . in part because he was so pleased and supportive. But with him now gone, I don't know . . . . . there's little joy in this work. Not now . . . . and I doubt ever," responds Luca, his voice trembling.

"So what do you want to do? Buy a winery?"

Elena's eyes glare at him, her face ghastly white against her black hair.

"Yes. Yes . . . . that's exactly what I want to do."

Luca takes another slow breath. Searches for the right words. Hopes Elena may be open to such a transition.

"I want to blend my chemistry training with the art of winemaking. I want to produce some excellent wines that will bring joy to people's interactions and lives. I want so much to create a wine that ignites greater happiness and consciousness rather than fear because of the problems I'm addressing. I really want to be happy . . . . like Grandad."

"And how do you propose to make that happen? Do you know a Genie who could help?" A sneer appears on Elena's face. "I hope you're joking, because I have no interest in such a venture," she says mockingly.

"Well, not a Genie. But . . . . I've been developing a plan."

Luca notices the tightness in his chest and attempts to relax. But rigid muscles do not release easily.

"Luca, if you go through with this, Angelo and I will return to New York. I grew up with uncertainty, never knowing how we would live with my father's unsteady jobs. I told you that when we got married. I can't . . . . I won't go through it again."

"Elena, please. Let's just talk this through. I have a good idea of how we can do this. And while money will be tight for a while, I'm pretty sure I can make this happen. I've been in contact with vintners in the area, and even a great consultant who said he would help us. I have experience from my grandfather's vineyards. And his old winemaker would help me. I really believe I can do this. Elena, I'm sure I can make it financially feasible."

"And what about the promise you gave me to make this position work, to keep the security of the university and academia. You have a great pedigree. If you just work harder, you CAN do this, Luca."

"It's one thing to work under stress and pressure from a dream job. It's another to do so from someone else's dream. It's Dad's dream and your dream I am trying to fulfill. Not mine. I can't do this the rest of my life, Elena. Not when I'm clear about what I really need to do."

"But you promised. Six years ago, you committed to me that you would stay with this career," shouts Elena.

"People change."

"And so do promises, apparently."

She glares at Luca, then shifts her gaze to the clenched fists against her thighs.

"People get clearer about not wanting to live out other people's dreams, whether it was Dad's or your's. I tried to keep my promise. It's killing me."

"Well, I don't think Napa suits the life I want to live."

"No, I think the life you want to live doesn't suit Napa."

"Well, I told you that if you didn't stay with this job, I would move back to New York."

She glares at him. Rises from the couch. Walks into the bedroom.

Luca's body remains in constant contractions, as he hoped their departure would not happen so quickly. He is speechless as she packs Angelo's belongings, watching her, with no idea of what else to say.

He spends more time at work where he is less likely to be in a constant state of tears. Yet, he knows he cannot stop Elena and believes his son needs his mother for the moment.

Elena keeps her promise and moves Angelo and herself back to her family home in New York City two weeks after their severing argument.

Luca continues his determination to change careers. During the only remaining conversations, the couple discuss terms for the divorce, child visitations, and the selling of their home.

Part of Luca sinks into that dark hole, an intermixing of sadness bordering on despair. He talks occasionally to Pablo, his friend in Napa. But mostly, he begins a meditation practice to help him stay clear about what most matters in his life.

What keeps blossoming during these slow breathing sessions are his connection with Angelo and the making of high quality wines. That part of himself, his determination to develop a Napa winery, remains strong.

With the summer off, he moves his things to a studio apartment, then prepares their home for sale. Once he finds an agent, he spends much of the summer in Napa.

Luca resides with Pedro, whom he knew as an adolescent and now works at the Oenophilia Winery in Yountville, a new establishment with promising wines. He obtains a part-time job helping there in the vineyards and barrel room while also attending viticultural classes at UC Davis.

When not studying his wine books, he drives around checking different parts of the valley for soil types, differences in microclimate, and possible hillside vineyards, just as Warren Winiarski did before discovering a location in the Stag's Leap area for his winery.

Luca's body feels the increase in physical labor and long hours, more corporeal than in his academic job. But his inner darkness begins to lighten. Joy gradually returns to his life.

He spends time writing Angelo letters once a week, puts the messages in a safe box, for his son to read later about how much his father always loved and missed him. If Elena warms to the idea, he will begin mailing them or delivering them when he visits New York.

By late August, Luca drives back to Southern California. He enjoys the area, but he also realizes his heart remains in Napa. It's another confirmation of his decision to shift careers.

Shortly after the school year begins, he resigns his contract effective at the end of the academic year. Luca notices anxiety about giving up a great position. Yet, his relief and excitement far outpace his fear.

The department chair soon relieves Luca of his research facility, making it available for a new hire. Such action provides this instructor, now having both feet out of the lab, more opportunity to study wine making. His dean assigns an additional class to teach, replacing some research responsibilities. But it is one he taught before and will not take extensive efforts.

His house sells quickly. Half the profits get deposited into his account while the other half go to Elena.

Once the academic year ends, Luca moves what little he still owns to Napa Valley. He finds a small apartment and works again at Oenophilia in order to gain additional experience.

He becomes adept at pruning vines, plowing the vineyard, and pre-dawn harvesting, as he did with his grandfather many years ago. The wine student learns the dirty art of cleaning tanks and barrels, keeping everything sanitized.

The scent of fermented wine is reassuringly familiar, as are the cleaning fluids. In the evenings, he talks with other vineyard workers, managers, and wine makers about their craft. A small notebook appears frequently to incorporate information he wants to remember.

At the end of the night, he often considers, before going to sleep, how his commitment to himself transformed his life from one struggle to another. But the latter produces more joy.

Still, he misses Angelo immensely. His son remains too young to hold an emotional conversation. Talking to Elena or her family helps little.

When he can't talk to Luca, he sits down and writes him another letter. He now mails them to himself so it contains a date stamp. He shares what is happening in the development of his winery, his sadness that Angelo is so far away, his love for both his son and creating quality wines. When a letter arrives, he tosses it in the box.

In early December, he receives the final disposition papers from his parent's estate. Luca opens the envelope and stares at the summary page, moving it further away, then closer, to make sure he reads the total amount correctly. The figures never change. He sets the paper on the table in front of him and leans back in his chair.

The Genie emerges from the envelope. His inheritance climbed to three times the amount Luca thought his parents had accumulated.

Luca pulls the pad of paper on the table towards him and starts writing down his new plan. He will put money into an account to cover his child-support payments and money for Angelo's college. He will put some in savings and possible investments to cover winery and travel costs. But the bulk he will try to leverage into a small vineyard, hopefully containing a home and barn he could use to make his wine.

He takes a deep breath. Hope and his parents transformed his reality.

The next day he inquires of Pedro.

"Do you know a good agent who could help me acquire a piece of vineyard land?"

"Yes, I do. Wynston. He helped us with our place and was excellent. Knows a lot of people in the valley and hears of off-market places too. I'll have him call you."

Within weeks, Wynston finds a distressed 23 acre property the owners need to sell due to financial difficulties. They seem amenable to a slightly lower price while still including basic farming and winemaking equipment. Within a month, he completes the transaction.

The old, rough, white paint peeling house requires lots of work. It is livable for one with no ascetic taste. More importantly, the barn remains sturdy and provides ample space for initial winemaking. Luca worries less in the moment about the home and needed repairs. His focus lies with the quality of the vineyard along with a covered space for fermentation and aging of his precious libation.

Luca sublets his apartment and moves into his new home. With his heart still tender from the divorce, it inflates as he steps into his own vineyard. His eyes scan the equipment. His excitement sours, even with the needed preparation before the fall harvest.

He sits on his porch the first morning after the move, recalling the dinners at his grandparents table. His Nonna would create amazing smells in her kitchen, the culinary cuisine embraced by big bowls or platters on the table. His granddad would open his wine, pouring some for each. Even Luca could have one small glass with water added for the toast before dinner. Then they would talk about what each smells and tastes in the wine. Luca never recovered from such explorations of wine.

The summer breeze through the screen door cooled them off. The laughter blew the other way, out to the back porch and into the vineyard. The fabulous marinara sauce with fresh mushrooms and basil over the chicken parmesan always made his mouth water.

As Luca took his first drink of tasty Zinfandel, Granddad would wink. He somehow knew this young man felt at home here. The memories nurture his hopes and the increasingly tangible realities.

Luca faces the hardest work he has done in his life, except when he hauled the full bins of grapes over to the wagon in his grandfather's vineyard. His doctoral and lab work began to feel like an ancient dream and physically uncomplicated in comparison.

At the same time, his heart increasingly sings, accompanied at times by his voice in an old Italian aria. He prunes the vines during the dormant winter, preparing for the spring that will regenerate life back into the rootstock. He gains new ideas from André Tchelistcheff's St. Helena seminars, often staying after to ask questions and share gratitude for the assistance. Other vintners offer ideas and advice in creating his first vintage.

As the rains diminish and the sun stimulates the blossoms, tragedy strikes. His well runs dry.

Like many others before him, Luca contacts a recommended Water Dowser, Fernando, who uses two rods to identify promising locations for well drilling. His scientific mind doubts the process and likelihood of success. But Pablo swears by the man, having personally witnessed him locate four different wells in the valley. The man charges less money than geologists. Several say he's more accurate. So Luca decides to explore this possibility.

Fernando comes three days later and walks the property.

"You have two promising sites for a new well," Fernando tells Luca and Pablo, who desires to hear any news about potential water. "One is near the house and would be convenient for the winery. The other lies at the top of the vineyard and would allow more gravity to provide water to both vines and buildings. This also may be part of an underground spring. I recommend trying that upper location first."

"That's great news," responds Pablo while shaking the dowser's hand with both of his. "Thanks so much, Fernando. Hopefully, we don't have to drill too deep."

Drilling begins a week later. Luca can hardly breathe. He worries that he will find nothing there to sustain the vineyard.

Strong winter rains soaked the ground, providing nourishment during the spring. But without a well during the dry season, a good crop becomes less likely. Yet, hope springs eternal with Luca. Challenges continue to be solved.

Luca tries to work on repairing equipment and getting barrels imported for harvest. He cleans the four tanks, soaking himself as part of the learning process. He then moves to three large bins that will ferment the grapes before moving the wine into the barrels for aging. Yet all may be for naught without water to nurture the fruit.

When the digging crew finds water, Luca breathes again. Lots of water permits extended breath. The testing indicates the water is clean and need not be filtered. In fact, the water tastes better than any he remembers.

He has a large tank placed at the top of the vineyard for his drip system, a much more efficient way to water than his grandfather's irrigation and sprinklers. A pipe is run to the two large tanks already located near the barn and house. As he watches the last pipes get attached and tested by the end of the month, he notices the tightness in his chest relaxes and hope increases.

Knowing he will need help, Luca hires a young couple, Heidi and Joe, to help work the vineyard and winery. They have experience in wine growing and fermenting, providing additional ideas to his venture. He hires a vineyard consultant to advise them about the vines and Andre for winemaking. He also obtains useful suggestions from other small vintners in the valley, like David Long, who recently planted the first vineyard on the west side of Pritchard Hill.

By fall, the fruit increases its readiness for harvest. The levels of brix are about what he is seeking. The grapes are abundant and producing a lovely flavor. Pablo and another close friend volunteer to help Luca and his hired couple reap the fruit and sort the grapes. The process comes together as Luca envisioned after constant efforts in learning and labor. Soon the fermentation will begin, followed by aging in the barrels.

As Luca stands by the crush conveyor belt sorting out green grapes and leaves that got into bins, a voice calls out from below.

"Could you use any more help?" asks a dark haired woman, her hair pulled back into a ponytail, a straw hat shading her face, in Levis and a plaid shirt.

As Luca looks into her dark eyes, something familiar peers back at him.

"Hi there. Yes, we probably could. But I can't pay much," responds Luca with a broad smile.

"André sent me over. My name is Sofia. He said you might be able to use another hand and maybe some help with winemaking. I've been working with him for three years now. I'm looking for some additional experience, which is more essential than a big paycheck."

"Well, then, you've come to just the right spot. Hop up here and get your hands dirty. This is Heidi, next to you, and that's Joe down there moving the stems around. This is my dear friend, Pablo. Now I'm even more indebted to André. I may need your insight as to the best way to repay him," chuckles Luca.

The crush goes more smoothly with one more set of hands. The juice and must get into the cleaned out tanks and bins.

Five days later, after the third pump over in the tanks and punching the caps in the bins, Luca is ready to eat and relax. His dream steadily becomes his reality, with all the effort it takes to transform the conceptual to physical. His excitement balances his exhaustion.

He has completed his first crush and soon will begin the second press. Every step brings new information, experience, and confidence in the maceration and fermentation processes.

His thoughts turn to Sofia again, noticing how easy it is to be with her. He admires her knowledge of both vineyard care and suggestions for working with the wines. Maybe having her over for dinner from time to time would help with what he will owe her.

His thoughts turn back to an unexpected aspect that appears in his transmutation. He felt pride in what he accomplished in his research lab and the connection his work made with his father. Yet, he realizes now that his contributions came from a desire to please more than a genuine desire to do the work.

In his current incarnation as a winemaker, he does not focus on saving lives. But his product can bring people together in celebrations, conversations, and interactions from a more authentic self. Recently, he feels the same thing about his own interactions, efforts and discussions.

This may not be *life-saving* work. Yet, he experiences this contribution now as a *life-living and giving vocation.*

Creating excellent wine presences himself with himself and others. Luca realizes he feels more alive and full of passion for living and sharing with these endeavors. This life facilitates happiness that can be extended to others who desire to participate and benefit from a simple energetic and chemical transformation.

He also senses that the joy he experiences is not just a mental thought, but rather a full body sensation. Such work contrasts dramatically from his academic exercises.

These body sensations and the contrast to abstract concepts in his head become the crux of what he wants to pass on to his son. After dinner, he sits down to write a long letter to Angelo, expressing his thoughts and feelings. He shares himself and his own life lesson for a future conversation with his son. He also shares some of his grandfather's observations as they experienced a sip of his latest, and as it turns out, his last vintage.

"Taste the earth's expression of hope. Savor the possibilities, as the taste of the wine lingers in your palate and your throat," his grandfather once advised him. "Pay attention to how it lingers, long beyond your last swallow. That's the mark of a good wine and a good relationship. Your grandmother's taste still lingers after all these years."

Some day, he hopes Angelo will spend time here, developing similar memories that Luca felt in the vineyards as a boy. He may even feed off of the joy from his granddad when the two would taste another satisfying vintage, the culmination of their loving labor.

Then he wonders if his son might also enjoy being around Sofia.

Wine Memories
Marianne Lyon

A graceful swirl
of Cabernet
dervishes me down
to Grandpas' cellar
dark   shrouded
pungent
sweaty barrels
stained red

A coquettish
swirl
of Chardonnay
and
I feel his
velvet eyes smile
through legs
transparent
dancing around
the glass

I sip
Pinot Noir
recline
impromptu
in Provence vineyard
Taste lacy flowers
waltzing
with wild fruit

disco swirl
whiff
aerated memories
another sip

buttery memories
still to be fermented

Writing Prompts 9

1. Pick a job or career choice you have imagined and admired. How would somebody shift to that career in your mind? How would that work? What would it take? Would that imaginary person be happier or dissatisfied with the change in the end?

2. Think about a time in your life when you couldn't make a decision. Write a story or poem based on that difficult situation and the feelings that arose or might have arisen at the time.

3. Write about something you don't want to do and what you would rather do instead.

4. Use the last line of one the poems ("regeneration" or "buttery memories still to be fermented") as the inspiration for the first line of your poem.

5. Write a story or poem about a shift or change that can take you somewhere different than where you are now.

CHAPTER TEN

Conflicts

As you read the short story and poems in this chapter, consider the following:

Do you have an inner voice? What does it tell you?

My Conviction Collision
Geoffrey K. Leigh

My stomach churns, nausea increases. The critical comments darken my world, despite the inky fragrance of new and musty scented used books crammed into ceiling tall cases.

Many attendees provide supportive responses to the reading from my new book, <u>The Spiritual Benefits and Limits of Organized Religions</u>. The manager of my local bookstore, where I conduct the reading, seems excited about the work that sheds light on an increasingly popular perspective. She packed in extra white padded folding chairs to augment the attendees comfort.

Over half the audience asks thoughtful questions and appear interested. Several express appreciation for my analysis. Others share additional examples from their own personal experience. Following the final applause, many wait in line to purchase autographed copies.

Yet, an angry response, two poisonous questions, and twin hecklers impugn the suggestion I made that organized religions primarily limit spiritual growth. Their comments hang in my ears throughout my interactions with the patrons who stay behind.

My blue tattered jacket covers my sweaty white shirt. Regular jeans feel confining. I'm relieved when I complete the last signing, thank the owner and wander to my car.

On my 20 minute drive home, I attempt to relax with each breath. Yet, the anchor on my heart drags any satisfaction to the depths, where it becomes covered by my mental seaweed, kelp and rockweed.

I anticipated a few attendees might get emotional about my organizational challenges. I described examples of perceived limitations to all the world's major religions.

Before entering the bookstore, I attempted to mentally prepare myself for some disgruntled attendees. They might not want to hear examples people from very different backgrounds reported through my interviews and surveys. My anticipation included attendance by some reactionaries. I underestimated how easily they would rock me.

Upon my return home, I park in the garage and enter the kitchen. The stale scent of broccoli from last night's dinner hangs in the air, adding to my contagious nausea.

I extend a hand against the island, unclear where to go. To the bedroom and change clothes, to the bathroom and regurgitate this experience, or straight to my wine cellar for an aged Petite Syrah to dilute the acerbic taste in my mouth. I decide on the initial, followed by the final option.

Now wearing more comfortable black sweats, an old gray t-shirt and worn tan slippers, I pour myself a glass of wine. I walk toward the back of my home and settle into my overstuffed brown chair in the garden room. There I can commune with my ficus, rubber plant, jade, and parlor palms, my luxuriant friends.

Since I enclosed my patio to create a climate controlled atmosphere with windows all around, I love the verdant surroundings of my plants. They revel to have me near. Freshen the atmosphere. I provide them carbon dioxide to nourish their growth. They continue the enhancing exchange.

The fabric and stuffing embrace me as I sink into the chair. Yet, the criticism finds innovative ways inward, continuing to twist my joy into discouragement and initiates the sink into a familiar dark hole. The derogatory comments flourish and dismiss any positive responses.

My mind spins, my gut hurts. I notice my chest tighten as the mental contractions increase. I had convinced myself I prepared for possible negative reactions, knowing conceptually not to take them personally. Reminiscing on the angry, contorted faces, any remaining strength wanes.

As I take another sip of wine, an internal voice not previously noticed begins to telepath thoughts with me.

"Paradise and Hell   oft distant destinations

yet current interactions manifest the latter's present experience
forged by people from judgments and anger
surrounding you with contracted perspectives."

I cannot recall accessing such an internal sharing of information in my life, even in the deepest of my meditations. Any prior inspirations that occurred with my writing or insights through contemplations have felt like an entrance from some locale external to myself. Now, this intruding voice appears to emerge from a source within me, some place other than my mind.

I don't understand what you're saying, I respond mentally to this poetic utterance. *Are you trying to tell me something?*

"Sorrow and joy show up to face you
Your focus comes from choice
When you allow another option
you can wallow in the mud or fly with the birds."

As the words wash over me, my stomach knot tightens. Rather than clarity, confusion reigns.

I relax further into my chair, take another sip of wine, uncertain how to respond and uneasy with this unripe interaction.

Who are you? Why are you whispering to me? What are you trying to tell me?

"When cold winds blow
a plant sinks roots deeper
holding its ground against the air
that whisks around loose leaves"

Confusion escalates. The points remain vague and this novel source amplifies my discomfort.

I decide maybe a dip in my hot tub will help relax me and dissolve the inner annoyances.

I stand and open one of the sliding doors to the rest of my garden, providing fresh air. I place my wine glass on the table aside the garden room tub, remove my clothes, pull the top back from the how water, then step inside.

The warm liquid nuzzles my skin. I bring it up in cupped hands to douse the top of my head. The heat helps my body soften as I suspire several times. I rub my fingers across my scalp and through my thinning hair, while continuing to breathe slowly.

Yet, all this does not cleanse away the inner voice.

"Breathe life into your multiverse body.
Wash the physical surface as energetic extensions loosen restrictions
Look with poetic eyes   more possibilities
Allow options not previously noticed
Let your soul fashion a sensual opportunity
Great heights can expand your vision."

Am I going crazy? Have I stepped over the edge? What the hell is going on with me? What's wrong with me?

I plug my nose and lower my body into the tub. Hot liquid engulfs me. As I come up for air, the jets turn on, pulsating my tender skin. The warm steam arising from the water clears my nostrils. I continue to hope the darting water will settle both mind and body.

When this strange speaker no longer continues to opine, I sit up straight and take a big breath. My body relaxes in this liquid environment. My mind decides what to do next.

I reach for my stemware placed on the table next to the tub. Take another sip, followed by a second. I allow the libation to pervade my palate.

I replace the glass, then step out and dry myself. Slipping back into casual clothes, I grab three pillows and decide to meditate.

Maybe that will help clarify what's going on with me, I reflect wistfully.

As I cross my legs and take slow deep breaths, my shoulders lower, my mind gradually goes blank. A wave of calm overtakes me. I begin to feel increasingly present with myself and perceptibly aware of every body part.

Through the silence, the voice reemerges.

"Yes, breathe in the breath of life, sending timeless love to your soul
Open the door to the core of your being
Step thoroughly through the opening
Caress the spark that connects to all"

I shake my head. Yet, the movement fails to wobble or disrupt the inner voice. At the same time, the words begin to make eerie sense, stimulating a simultaneous curiosity.

Is it the voice or the information that's most disturbing? I ask myself.

The mental disorder created by the voice shifts to disequilibrium, which amplifies my discomfort.

I suspire one more time, allowing my attention to shift from the orator to the ideas being expressed. I can't recite the exact words. Yet, the general concept begins to seep into my being. More specifically into my chest.

I intend a breath of fresh air towards my heart, inviting it to expand, increase its opening as I have frequently practiced. With such an invitation, my shoulders lower further as I relax my back against the wall.

Are you me or some external voice, a separate being? I ask.

"How do you separate your air from others
your thoughts from other perspectives
Are you such a detached individual
that you share nothing with anyone else

Are you so disconnected from life
Is the door to your loving core so closed"

Of course I'm not completely separate, unique and unconnected from every-
one else. But how do I deal with those who get so angry at what I have to say?
Who heckle and taunt me? They seem to want to destroy me and my point of
view.

"Fruits and flowers, plants of all types thrive on manure and putrescent
vegetation
The stench is greatest as it begins to turn
Don't get caught up in the malodor from others
You lose focus of your concepts and convictions."

I sit quietly. The words again douse over me. I begin to see how my
focus narrows to anything negative, contractive, and unpleasant. While
new ideas also can make me uneasy, there is expansion and excitement
when I intumesce to incorporate a fresh perspective. But I constrict around
a criticism of me or my work. I narrow my vision to occupy only the
contraction.

OK, I see what you are saying. I know new ways of thinking or acting are
uncomfortable for many people. I forget how much they can make me pull
back, feel uneasy. But what should I do? How do I prevent that?

"People need time and love to incorporate new ideas and alternative per-
spectives
Provide space and support free of judgment
Love and sugar attract more than hate and vinegar"

That's it? Love them without judgment? Not so easily done. I wished you
had a more helpful suggestion.

"Life is a practice
perfection not required
Breathe love out and in"

That sounds easy, but I don't find it so simple. I get caught up in my reactions. They hold me. It's not easy to let them go.

"Rhymes   riddles   mind games
can assist you in breaking
self constructed box"

Realizing I'm no longer meditating, I get off my pillows and move back to my encapsulating chair. I take a deep breath, my focus on the voice's last rejoinder.

You're suggesting I play with my responses, especially with others?

"Unexpected reciprocations   enjoyable rebuttals
can lessen reactions to a new view
Something lighter   even lovingly playful
eases tensions when newness elicits contractions
Core love can open many locked doors"

I savor these last few comments, allowing them to permeate my being, particularly my heart. I have known these points conceptually. I am familiar with the ideas. Increasingly, it all makes logical sense. But I have not assimilated these into a life practice.

I don't hold on to love when criticism emerges, or when it's in my face. I allow other people's perspectives and emotional anger, especially if it incorporates rage, to supersede my own beliefs and emotions.

"Yes, other views are important to consider while retaining your own foundation

until it is time to shift or incorporate pieces that are important for your ease and growth"

I guess the key is to inspect and evaluate other points of view rather than letting them simply replace what I have built. It's just tricky to know when to listen and when to defend.

"If your creation brings ease
defense is a reaction
Let love be your vibe"

I breathe in this remark, feeling the truth in it. As I exhale, I realize my next task, or rather practice.

Inhaling another breath, I visualize love as I take in life giving oxygen, then exhale adulation for my plants that feed from my release. I inhale gratitude, then make a whooshing sound as I exhale love towards the jade plant closest to me.

I get up and do the same exercise with each of the other plants. I focus on the adoration for the lushness, richness, beauty, and joy each brings daily to me. I treasure the fertile atmosphere they provide. As I sit back in my chair, gratitude expands my body.

Now will you tell me who you are? Where do you source this inspiration?

"What do you holistically view when you look deep inside
Is there something just beyond the dark hole
Is there an opening in you or a mirage
At some level, everything is connected as all parts of your body are linked
Am I you talking to yourself
Or are you me playing out my intentions

We are that part of us that is joined with all"

I sit with increasing peace and amazement. Love and gratitude begin to permeate my being. I want to believe what this voice has just shared. That will take time. It will require repetition. Yet, there may be no better practice that I undertake than this one.

And can we laugh at this, too? I feel so good and such relief in this moment. I could almost do a laughing meditation. Roll on the floor. Chuckle at how long this has taken me in my life to feel the truth of these words. Even if there is much to exercise.

"A writer at times would shrink
When people remarked his works stink
Then he found his core voice
Providing him with more choice
Now he just gives them a smile and a wink"

Writing Prompts 10

1. Consider writing a found poem from this previous piece. You could use just the prose section, the poetry sections, or all of it.

2. Write a found poem in prosetry format.

3. Choose 5 words from the above Section 10. Write a poem with those words contained in the verse.

4. Write a poem or story using this sentence as your opening line: *Who are you? Why are you whispering to me? What are you trying to tell me?*

5. Write a poem or a short story in response to:

> *"How do you separate your air from others*
> *your thoughts from other perspectives*
> *Are you such a detached individual*
> *that you share nothing with anyone else*
> *Are you so disconnected from life*
> *Is the door to your loving core so closed"*

CHAPTER ELEVEN

Memories

As you read this chapter, consider the following:

What does Metamorphosis mean to you?

Goody Two Shoes
Marianne Lyon

Don't want to be a goody two shoes.
Played the role, begged for approval
chose it for decades
Missed out on too many struggles
promising miracles
Like the way she takes second in spelling bee
her frown and saddened eyes
lift to my First-Place glittering gaze
Like how I don sainthood, palms just so
for morning prayers and
sister elects me to clean incensed sanctuary.
While they play a ruckus game of dodgeball
red-faced, giggles loud as a hurricane
I only envision firefly gaiety
Sanctified dust rag weeps from my limp hands

I want to go back to that playground
a delight to even imagine
wild Cheshire smiles bidding me
luxuriate in ball-bouncing frivolity
a delight to even
be drawn into their clustered joy
from sideline of unattainable perfection
miraculous   encircled
in bright dancing carnival
not doing anything special   simply being
It's   I know   dreaming
but I am aging   not much more time

Allow me this sweet fantasy

My Hourglass Life
Geoffrey K. Leigh

<u>My Early Years</u>

About the age of 35, I made a series of decisions that dramatically changed my life. I didn't know at the time how much they would transform my world. I felt very hemmed in and needed to make a shift to survive. Now, at age 74, I can see how expansive that turning point was, allowing more breath in my lungs, more freedom in my movements, more relaxation in my throat, more creativity in my expression, more opening of my heart, and more gratitude for life.

As I recall, I had a happy childhood, even into the first few years of elementary school. My mother was a teacher. But while I was young, she taught part-time at a preschool I attended down the block. I had friends from my preschool years that ended up graduating in the same high school class, although most of us were not as close as in those early days.

When not at preschool, I played with my Fort Apache set, drove my little cars in the dirt, and listened incessantly to Sergei Prokofiev's 1946 original English recording of Peter and the Wolf, narrated by Sterling Holloway. My mother turned over the 78 rpm records time and time again. I'm sure she said to herself, "when will he get tired of this?" But she continued to cooperate, partly because it involved classical music, which she loved.

My own appreciation of such music grew out of that repetitive story, as well as a life-long phrase among friends, "Here we go, through the snow, comrades forever." Ironic that I learned and loved the phrase while growing up in the anti-communist atmosphere of the 1950s.

I also decided early in life that being a mail delivery person may be in my future.

"Here is your mail, ma'am," I would say as I handed my mother empty envelopes out of my proud old leather satchel. Then I would deliver more to many chairs and other "post office boxes" around the living and dining rooms. Afterwards, I would circulate to pick them up, asking my mother, "do you have mail to be delivered ma'am?" It was a fine delivery service, although I believe my mother tired of the frequency. Collecting mail every 3-5 minutes may be a little relentless.

When my sister was home, she needed a partner for her creative dance practice. Given my older brother's lack of interest, I was the inducted male partner. I learned to move my body in interesting ways, to stretch, to test my muscles, and to experience the music throughout my body. The biggest downside with this and later tap, I never could spin without upsetting my stomach. But I could get very dramatic, which she loved, was rather creative, and, thanks to her, learned to love dancing.

My dad traveled quite a bit, and my older brother and sister were in school much of the day. That left me at home to find chocolate bunnies my sister was saving, which satisfied my sweet tooth, along with the endless small cups of raisins that needed refills constantly. We finally got a television, which meant I could watch the Mickey Mouse Club Show and my first cartoons, although my mother insisted I do other things, too.

Until I learned to read myself, one of my favorite evenings were Sundays, when I could sit next to my father, when at home, as he read about how "Lightfoot the deer" would get into mischief and danger. I later included a wider variety of Burgess and other books. Yet, those weekend evenings when my father was home reading were favorites.

With my neighbor, Val, we tried our hand at writing space adventure stories on small "books" of paper we made by cutting them into little notebook size sheets with a staple in the middle. It only took me about 60 more years to activate any confidence as a creative writer.

From time to time, my mom and I would take the Bamberger train from our home in Bountiful to Salt Lake City so she could do some shopping. While walking to the station or in the stores, my mother would say, "hurry along now, Geoffrey. You're walking too slowly," as my little legs could not keep up with her. About 10 years later as I grew to be almost a foot taller than Mom, it would be something more like, "slow down, Geoffrey. You're walking too fast!"

I didn't realize it at the time, but it was an early indicator of the changes that would take place in my life as my attitudes, values, and interests changed almost as dramatically as my height, just two decades later. But these early years were good memories with a general sense of happiness and fun.

A cornerstone of our family was the Mormon religion that had convinced ancestors on both my mother and father's sides of our family to leave Europe and come to the United States, roughly a century before my developing years. I didn't realize how central that history was in our family until I began to question aspects of it beginning in my adolescence.

In retrospect, much of the first half of my life was trying to please my parents, church, and a "God" that would love me IF I obeyed what his prophets told us to do. While my older brother was comfortable challenging the first two aspects and choosing a different way to please the Divine, I chose early patterns of silencing my voice, keeping things peaceful, and not 'rocking the boat.' So I willingly went to church, was proud of any church assignments, and kept any challenges quiet until high school.

Years later, my sister gave me a framed Norman Rockwell magazine cover.

"This reminds me so much of Mom and Dad," she said when handing it to me.

I agreed with her. There was my father, dressed for work reading the paper and my nicely dressed, hair perfect mother sitting at the breakfast table. That wasn't exactly our parents. But the essence of conformity was very much present. I believe it was the kind of picture our mother, who loved Rockwell's art, desired to paint with our family.

Gladdener*
Marianne Lyon

I try to please
parents   church
a God
who will love me
if I obey
prophets' words

Willingly
go to church
accept proudly
any assignments
any challenges
I quietly hide

My essence is
conformity
see myself on
a Norman Rockwell
magazine cover
next to my
perfect mother
perfect father
perfect home

Choose to silence
my voice
keep things peaceful
not   rock the boat

I sometimes think
we paint to supply things
we want and don't have – Norman Rockwell

*A found poem from *My Early Years* by Geoffrey K. Leigh

Church
Marianne Lyon

"Really," you spit a jeer
"You   who haven't entered a vestibule in years
except to kneel before an ancient statue
or view a centuries-old relic"

If I were to erect a church
I should build it into a song

"Explain," you say smirking a grin

It would not be written on a staff
with sharps and flats
symphonic style, nor a concerto
It would be an improvisation
maybe a hint of jazz, a touch of spiritual

"Sacrilegious," you add with insult

Listen   hear lone voice hum a slow minor melody
another modulates   yodels a bright major
trio harmonizes a conversation invites
whole chorus of sounds to echo inside
deep forest smelling of sweet pine incense
no maestro conducts from gilded pulpit

"You've tangled my thoughts"

Voices multiply   begin to offer sonic liturgy

to every part of woodland concert hall
birds even start to tweet
squirrels stop their nut collecting

"Ridiculous!"

Few strollers jarred from their rumination
begin to listen   ponder this wordless song
wonder what this eerie construct means

<u>Roller Coaster Contractions</u>   (*My Hourglass Life* Continued)

When I moved into adolescence and young adulthood, I worked harder to connect with my dad, primarily because he felt more emotionally distant than my mom. Having both British ancestors and an engineering degree, it was a gap that was not easily traversed.

As I grew up, I remember his mother, who was born in this county, having hot tea every afternoon around 4:00. It was decades later that I realized she was continuing the British tradition of tea time, although she never lived in or visited England. Her husband served a Mormon mission there many years previously. He didn't live long enough for me to know if he shared in the practice.

In the end, my parents expected children to conform to their world rather than connecting through the perspective of the younger generation. And the "right" church seemed to make that even more of an appropriate expectation. Such demands were consistent with many previous generations, and I realized that conforming expectations were not limited to my religion.

My adolescent years began my 'Roller Coaster' relationship with the Mormon Church, my ups with conformity and my downs with rebellion. I wanted to be a 'good boy' so that God would love me, and, according to the church, conformity to the doctrine was the only way that could happen. Yet, I would struggle with issues, such as the teachings that African Americans could not hold the priesthood, which, according to some, was because they were being punished by God. There was a hierarchy of men over women, which I think bothered my mother, and it felt wrong to me.

I also would read more expansive ideas in the writings by B.H. Roberts, a Mormon philosopher, whom I found fascinating. Roberts was willing to explore new ideas and possibilities that were creative and less traditional. Yet, they were not accepted by the more conservative parts of that religion, which over time became the large plurality of church leadership and membership. As my views became more liberal, the schism expanded in my life, especially as I increased my education and national connections with colleagues.

Probably the most significant spiritual experience in my early life occurred at age 16. I remember the age because of the doctrine that Joseph Smith, the founder of the Mormon Church, was 14 years old when he reported a vision of God. I already was two years older than that, and I wanted confirmation that I was doing the right thing with my life too.

I was in my bedroom all alone, as my brother, who shared the room during my younger years, already was married and not living at home. I knelt down and prayed that I too might see God. I remember praying for quite some time, as a confirmation was very important to me. I suddenly experienced an overwhelming love energy and sense of bright light coming into my body, which I could hardly contain. Some time later, I woke up on my bed, not quite sure what happened or how long I was in the experience. I never 'saw God' with my literal eyes. But I never forgot that tremendous energetic feeling of love that I encountered for quite some time.

I also had no context to understand what I had gone through. I just knew I did not 'see God,' so I assumed it was not a divine experience or "revelation" by church standards. I simply continued to try conforming to the church to make sure I too was loved by the Divine being that I worshiped (the Roller coaster highs). At the same time, it set the stage for latter experiences that would lead me to more spiritual explorations while vacating the religious structure that held me early in life.

Despite that adolescent experience, I still had many challenges and questions or at times even disbelief that would make me want to distance myself from the church (the Roller Coaster lows). Even with my mission for the church, which was mostly a high, and my marriage in the temple, I continued to question whether it was the right thing for me. I was troubled by the race and gender hierarchies, which amplified during graduate studies and researching Feminism. Still, I would try to conform as much as I could and kept trying to participate as I was told to do.

Another interaction that portended my separation from the Mormon Church occurred during my adolescence. I had been thinking about people who were not part of the organization and "righteously inspired" by the church, people who seem to access accurate and conscious information while not part of the "true religion," such as that done by Edgar Cayce.

In speaking with another member, an older friend of my parents, I suggested, "Maybe as members, we simply are accessing an information source that may be available to all people on earth. Maybe there is a subtle source of information available to all humans when we learn to connect with it."

My older friend responded, "Accessing the truth from God or the Holy Spirit is only possible when we listen to our Prophet and obey the commandments of the one true church."

Interestingly enough, the idea I presented to her later blossomed into some of the basic ideas for which I found evidence to be accurate without any religion. This led to the writings in a book I published just a few years ago. Learning there was no room for alternative or new ideas increased my church challenges.

There are other examples of how I didn't really fit within the church structure. Upon returning from my mission in Switzerland for six months and Lebanon for 17 months, I gave my "report" to our ward or local congregation. While on my mission, I saw young people who didn't really want to be there and were less likely to contribute to the work. Some were promised cars or money if they went on a mission. Particularly in Utah, there was a status boost, especially for parents whose sons went on missions. So in my report, I recommended that young men and women only go if they were committed to the work. Unlike all the other missionaries in our area, I was never asked to talk in another ward or at larger gatherings.

No one told me directly, but I learned that if you don't talk the "party line," you're not invited to talk again. It was yet another place where I began to realize the Mormon Church was not a good fit for me. I could follow the church doctrine or follow my truth, but there was not room for both. I later chose my own spiritual path.

Once I was asked to talk in a church meeting. I had become fascinated by all the scriptural references to 'light' in the Bible. I went through and talked about these references, focusing especially on a scripture from John, where Jesus states, "I am the light of the world. Whoever follows me will never walk in darkness, but will have the light of life." I went on to speculate what these references might mean for us as 'children of God.' At the end of what I thought was the best religious talk I had given, only one member came up to share any feedback.

"Have you thought about voice lessons? The way you speak is annoying and turns people off," the member said. Years later, I realized that I spoke with a closed throat from all the years I had silenced my voice and so much of what I really wanted to speak out loud. I didn't realize it at the time, but that was the beginning of the end to my intellectual comfort with the Mormon institution.

Walk in the light
Marianne Lyon

I
Kneel
Pray

Energy
Overwhelms

I do not see God

Light
Fills
Me

I do not see God

Hear
I
Am
The
Light

I do not see God

Follow
Me
Never
Walk
In

Darkness

I do not see God

Metamorphosis*
Marianne Lyon

Deep struggle
separation   suffocation
buried   no survival

Somehow   I chose to shift
slowly began to breath
in a place where

No one made me
shut down
my voice

No one made me
worship
conditional God

No one made me
close off
emotions

No one made me
live only
in my head

Began
to discover
mind   body   wisdom

Began
to learn of life's gifts
deep relationships

Began
to expand   lead
live with open heart

*A found poem from *Transition Period* by Geoffrey K. Leigh

Transition Period   (*My Hourglass Life* Continued)

By age 36, I was in a deep struggle with my marriage and the church, which was important to my soon to be ex-wife. We were living in Iowa City, nearly 1200 miles from my parents. Within a year and a half, both my mother and then my father died unexpectedly, and I was denied early tenure at the University of Iowa, where I was teaching (although I was awarded tenure the next year).

That winter, as I recall, I asked my wife for a divorce. We had four wonderful children, and the separation that happened a year and a half later was difficult for all of us. But I felt like it was the only path that would give me breath and life.

My choices were suffocating me, which was no one's fault but my own. I was so accustomed to cutting off my voice and trying to keep the peace that I had created a path for which there seemed to be no survival. And while I missed my parents terribly and buried the stress that would take decades to unravel and recover, shifting directions gave me more freedom for self exploration and expanding my world. So began the eventual transition, with fallout along the way that I later tried to repair.

According to church authorities, which had provided a source of stability early in life, wanting a divorce was "selfish." Therefore, the institution was not supportive of my decision.

Following the separation, the local bishop asked me if he could take me to lunch for my birthday. Late in the meal, I found out the real reason he asked me to join him. Someone had seen me at lunch with a friend, who also was married. Because I was separated but still married at the time, he told me, "This is inappropriate behavior and you should stop."

Finding my voice after returning to my office, I went back to him. I suggested that what I would stop was my participation in the church. From that time on, I was free from the confines of what, for me, was a rigid institution.

After that decision finally to leave, I found myself able to begin breathing again. While the lunch conversation was the trigger point, the decision was long in coming.

After that experience, I began following what would become my 'spiritual' rather than a 'religious' path. It also ended my roller coaster relationship with the church, a decision I have never regretted.

One of the great gifts of my divorce was to bolster my exploration into my personal development, which I had begun with some experiential Gestalt work with a dear friend in the mid 1970s. With no one else to blame (one big down side of a divorce), I began to take more responsibility for my own issues and challenges.

No one made me shut down my voice, which made it difficult to hold my own in relationships, or conform to a conservative religious institution. No one made me worship a God who loved conditionally, one that would only care about or "bless" me if I did the 'right' thing within the institution in which I had chosen to participate. No one made me get married more out of fear than passion, although it seemed like a good idea at the time. No one made me shut off my emotions in order to live almost completely in my head.

During that period of striving for success in academia, a body seemed like a good thing to get my head/brain from one place to another, maybe playing a little along the way.

One dear friend during that period said to me, in the nicest way possible, "I've never met anyone more emotionally shut down than you."

It was true, of course, at the time, which is one reason I began to 'study' emotions academically. If there is something to explore, I would lead with my brain, of course. Fortunately, I later learned to include my body and eventually try to lead with my heart, dramatically expanding my experience in this world. I am so appreciative of such loving feedback. It effectively broadened my journey in this life.

The other great gift from my marriage was becoming a father. My former wife and I have four lovely children. They eventually married and had children themselves, giving the family nine wonderful grandchildren.

My oldest child came early in my life (age 23), and I was not prepared for fatherhood. I was still in school with years of graduate education ahead of me. With the later pressure on becoming tenured and developing connections with colleagues within academia, much of my focus was outside the home.

At the time, I thought my friends and colleagues were a primary source of learning about life. There were lots of discussions about people, a changing world, and current issues that I found stimulating and exciting. It took me two decades to realize my family was my greatest source of learning about children, life and love.

My polyphonic self
Marianne Lyon

From a bygone place
alto voice enters
slowly   angrily
from nowhere
long suspended oozing
she wails
you are not enough
another voice joins conversation
she sings   sounds
like child-castrato dotted on
You are music   radiant
moving   magnificent
crunchy   pungent dissonances
more unresolved phrases resound
keep me hanging on   hanging on
then   ahh   all at once   two voices
Inadequate and *Aplenty*
resolve argument
icicles melt magically
first   they are thick   opaque
lengthening   but mysteriously
they begin to glitter like
pieces of heavy glass
for a long moment   self-love
drips over the three of us

Still Have Time*
Marianne Lyon

Found
I can live my beliefs
quit hiding them
learned of
love
patience
creativity
authenticity
joy
all enlarged me

Discovered
consciousness
deep in my core
now   I am
grateful for
expansion

Still growing
still attempting
to live from my heart
to shine my light
that shines
for others

Still have some sand
left
in my hourglass

*A found poem from *Expanding My World* by Geoffrey K. Leigh

Expanding My World   (*My Hourglass Life* Continued)

My spiritual journey eventually included other traditions and points of view. I began a meditation practice and explored Tibetan Buddhism, later taking refuge in it. I later broadened my investigation through many different books, including those from channeled masters and works like *Conversations with God* by Neale Donald Walsch.

I then widened my search into energy fields, the near-death research reports, and our investigation into young children's abilities. I also spent time exploring my own defenses with another dear friend, Karen, and realized how young I was when putting my own patterns into place. This awareness helped me realize that children may bring much more into this world than we have given them credit or understood who they are beyond the physical/mental form.

I worried at first about how my evolving spiritual beliefs might impact my children, and I often kept those changes hidden. Later, I realized that I could live my beliefs and let my children choose their own. I never pushed my own practices on my children, but I quit hiding them too. As I became more comfortable and internalized more of my explorations, we could engage in discussions without pushing any particular tenant.

At the same time, my children and grandchildren became a primary learning influence about love, patience, creativity, authenticity and gratitude for of that enlarged my own world view, as well as the feedback and examples of the partners they brought into our family.

I moved further east for a few years early in my career to possibly my best academic position at Ohio State University. But that move made fact-to-face interactions with my children more difficult. They now lived in Utah with my ex-wife, and driving back and forth in December was not ideal. While I loved the job, I had little money to travel the 1700 miles to visit my kids.

Eventually, I found a job at the University of Nevada, Reno (UNR), which allowed me to be closer and spend more time directly with them. When I later moved to a Las Vegas office of UNR and the children became more independent, the interactions increased. Eventually, each of them came to live with me in Las Vegas at different times, which was a gift to my reconnecting process with them. It also was during that period that I was able to travel more and garner the ideas that would coalesce into my best work.

During my time living in Reno, in probably my favorite 'academic' style home, I also had a significant relationship with a woman, named Marianne. During this relationship, I meditated more consistently than I had, became vegetarian for both health, animal welfare, and to bolster my sacred path, and I focused more intently on my spiritual development. She was a strong support and blessing, although the relationship only lasted about four years. We reconnected several years later as 'Intimate Allies,' a deep and important friendship that continues to this day.

Slowly, my personal and professional explorations began to merge with our investigations into the energy fields of children in a preschool setting. During this time, I began a new personal relationship with Jean. It was a short and intense intimate relationship, which only lasted about two years. But it also began a professional relationship that led to my best research and laid the foundation for the integration of our work with many others exploring new frontiers.

This work culminated into my professional life's work with the publication of my book in 2017, *Rekindling Our Cosmic Spark: A Noussentric Approach to Living and Parenting*. While not every aspect of my life led to this publication, the main parts of my path assisted me in putting together the work of which I am most proud. Certainly the experience at age 16 that was re-experienced many years later and the ideas of accessing information available to all connected to this work that feels like my life's contribution.

Working on the *Rekindling* book for over two decades also helped me to transform early beliefs into my personal spiritual path. Following the examples of others, I learned to access intuitive and creative information that feels like it comes beyond my own thinking and mind.

Based on the thousands of near-death experiences and children's reports of past lives, I came to believe in reincarnation, a life before this existence where we make choices for this exploration. It also seems like we are here to learn and become more conscious, impacting not only our own being but those around us to whom we connect closely and influence.

Most important, I have a strong sense that at our core we are composed of a substance that sometimes is called love consciousness. This relates not only to my experience at age 16, but also provides more easily accessed spiritual experiences through meditations and altered states as an adult.

Following 30 years in academia, I decided to retire and move to California, a state that has been a draw for me all of my life. I moved to Napa Valley, which feels like a place where I am finally 'home,' more than any place I have lived, including where I was born.

My oldest daughter, Jen, also settled there prior to my move and was one motivation for moving to that area. While I also love the Seattle area, where Greg's family resides, the weather and feeling of Napa helps me feel more settled, more at home with the roots of the vines. Here I plan to remain. Now that Kati's family resides in Sonoma County, the roots dig deeper with my contentment nourishing them.

As I look back, I am grateful for the contractions that created security during an insecure period in my life, a time to get my feet planted under me in order to shift my path. At the same time, the transition at the most contracted point in my life provided a strong determination for expansion. In that process, I have accessed more creativity and a comfort with the lack of external structure, replacing it with my own choices of how I want to live and what I want to do.

In that enlargement of my options, I also have found a more stable inner self that has come back to that experience at age 16, knowing that the Divine is Unconditional Love, as I attempt to love my children and grandchildren.

I still am learning and growing, attempting to open and lead more from my heart. I feel more at home in this expansive place. I also desire that a creative, expressive self becomes the light of my life that shines to others. Fortunately for me, I still believe there is a little sand left in the hourglass. If so, I will keep writing.

Enoughness

Marianne Lyon

Enough came to me
been too weary to seek her
but she found me
always hoped
to know her deeply dreamed of her
now she is here

I need to go soon
She vocalizes

My teary eyes plead
I'm afraid I won't know what enough is
From her beating heart she drums

Say only enough words
think only enough thoughts
walk only enough walks
sing only enough songs
LOVE only enough people

My prayer hands supplicate

Please stay   sing   walk with me

Enough whispers

You have wise- enough guide

inside of you
trust her with your heart
She is strong sister to voices
all woman possess
must embrace
before any other voice
smile   listen   breathe   feel
feel deep   deeper yet
you know all the answers

She caresses my hands
you are enough

My Avocation   (*My Hourglass Life* Conclusion)

After moving to Napa and completing my book, I developed an interest in writing fiction. Although I enjoyed writing stories and poems in high school, I never saw myself as a fiction author. But the *Cosmic Spark* book stimulated the possibility of writing a novel connected to the ideas I had presented there.

While Kati was in high school and visiting me in Las Vegas, I asked her about writing a book for adolescents based on the ideas that eventually ended up in the 2017 publication.

"Should I publish a 'How To' book for adolescents or a fiction book?" I asked her.

She immediately responded, "Oh, a fiction book."

From that idea suggested 20 years previously, I developed my first novel.

While working in real estate, I began to see how 'staged' homes sell faster and for more money because some people have a hard time envisioning how they would live in an empty house. The fictional Noussentric Trilogy is still being created as my 'staged' books for *Cosmic Spark*.

Most fiction authors also write short stories as a practice in writing and way to become better known before starting a novel. In this case, I approached a writing career backwards. I started on my novel, never having any interest in writing short stories.

When I became involved with more writers in the Napa Valley, I also began to be inspired by ideas that could turn into stories. I realized that short stories could convey some of the ideas from *Cosmic Spark* in a variety of short examples and expressions.

I then began to work part-time hosting guests at David Arthur Vineyards. That encouraged me to create more stories and connect some to the life I love in Napa Valley, including my second novel. When I connected and became more impressed with Marianne's poetry, I loved the inspirations our interactions stimulated. This book emerged as I began to explore and practice writing in shorter forms and diverse formats.

I continue to experience an inner struggle to identify myself as a competent and interesting writer. Yet, I enjoy the creative process. I will continue to attempt improvement of my expression and reach for new methods and formats of sharing amorphous possibilities and articulations. I hope readers enjoy at least some of these writings.

Writing Prompts 11

1. Write a poem or short story to yourself, asking "What is left in my hourglass of life?"

2. What does Metamorphosis mean to you? Write about a memory of this happening in your life.

3. Write a story (a short story or even an Haiku) about someone in your life that went through a metamorphosis. What was it like for them?

4. Look outside your window. How are you connected to what you see?

5. Do you feel enough? Invite her into your life. Write about the two of you seeing each other for the first time.

Enough came to me
been too weary to seek her
but she found me
always hoped
to know her deeply
dreamed of her
now she is here

CHAPTER TWELVE

Grace

As you read the pieces in this chapter, consider the following:

What is a style of writing you never considered before now?

Memoir of Loving Gratitude
Marianne Lyon

I meander through the forest
west of the town where I grew up
a continent of light and shadow
trees have always been inside of me

I am lost in the smell of pitch that reaches out and surrounds me. Songs drip down wrinkled bark. Everyday family tunes spin, beckon memories. Here's the chokecherry patch where berries hang swollen. Wild genesis of Aunt May's sweet wine. There's my family's favorite picnic table. Once it poured so hard I thought the rain was wailing. Here's Rock Creek, water squeezing through boulders. Low trees bend down in a whispering.

In the distance is Silver Lake where dad fished for Rainbow Trout. A calm surface, a sheet of copper. Above, the rock pushes out from the mountain cliff. In summer Mom said it looked like the face of Jesus. I want others to step into extraordinary wildness, lope on moist floor of soft needles, hear hum of insects like ripples, wait near a gentle thread of stream where fish leap like rainbows.

He whistles through
the yards of his day
echoes charming birdsongs
whines ruckus Croatian ditties
deep in the realm of his
own melodic invention
tender toots
match his swagger
from garage
lucid trills give shape to

another project

Lately, I try to whistle, match Dad's timbre. Crinkle my lips. Vary moist curl of my tongue. Find a crevice between front teeth, but clouds of spit skirl out like an oscillating table fan. Insistent, I linger over a book given to whistling. Relentless scores of tunes intricate as an aria fly, soar, dive, dance wild tangos with haughty staccatos. Bach would be impressed that lips alone can maneuver such virtuosity and to carve, whittle, garden, walk at the same time.

I remember how each day he nobly pipered home, lunch bucket swinging a steady pulse. Certain in his course, his limbering form twists up narrow alley, lips purse, head tilts, I hear his signature tight high tootle unravel. Transfixed, I drop my crayons, run to the luxurious exhale.

> An autumn sun climbs over the Rockies
> spilling like a yoke onto the clouds
> mom's face awash with light
> her limp plumpness
> dozes in the Lazy boy rocker
> I wonder when she came to know
> the collection of words
> that would quiet, inspire, humble

They came out as a whisper of suggestions, *"If you can't say something nice...."* a jumble of sugary words sprinkle around me. Frustration and pride mix in. I choose *"don't say anything at all."*

They had an energy all their own, *"Don't cry over spilt milk"* pours me in paradoxical directions. I wasn't crying, didn't tip over my glass, yet the words empty my head. I could breathe again.

Mom sheltered me from the cruelty of the world. *"She needs to be taken down a few pegs."* An impressionistic blur, I only heard *down*. My rude friend was going down!

She was her words as much as her chubbiness, walking in the messiness of life. I feel fragments of these moments tumbling haphazardly in my mind. When her words expanded my sense of what was possible, *"the sky's the limit."* I just knew by the inflection, intonation, wide smile I had no fences back then.

Your golden filaments still textured me
glint in my memory of sunny afternoons
Where are you now, yellow couch?
Reupholstered, a costume change
a bed for a weary traveler?

I drop in your lap, the sorcery of you holds me soft. You sigh, tell me stories of vanished decades, a narrative that runs backwards like a magic river. You tell me of Christmas morning pictures, sister's baby doll, brother's red tracker, my Blue Willow tea set—a miniature of Grams.

I cuddled you during Saturday morning cartoons. Heckle and Jeckle wing from limb to limb taunting our ears. My marrow vibrates with ruckus giggles. A stinky fart explodes. My fiddly feet grab your brocade skin. We leap into forbidden jumping wilderness.

You hold her in a world of fabric and curve. I have no idea that day would be mom's last lying on you. She melts like salt in a sea of foam. You were her buoyant raft of safety, felt her breath slowing. A weak current of her life letting go.

You do not have to
do anything to be loved
you do not have to perform
or achieve
or earn a merit badge

> this needs to be repeated
> over and over
> be who you are
> love what is before you

I didn't have children, but if I did, I would tell them to be courageous. Be their own hero. Embrace friendships, release fear and unworthiness. Laugh even when they can't remember why. I would tell them to be a doggie, a hell raiser, wiggling, inquisitive, wordless, passionate for a rub, a treat, a ball-catch. Not to be worried about next spring. Want to tell them to be awake, a trailblazer. To scoff illusions that keep them believing what they see in the world is gospel, that keep them from recognizing the truth that lies underneath. Want to tell them about my childhood door.

> It may have been a hum
> a small voice
> a persistent hymn
> a gentle nudge
> that bid me step through
> the threshold to God

A high dusty window in our basement surveys a make-shift orphanage. Dolls swaddled in afghans, cradles rocking painted eyelids swung closed.

The sun, a bright disc hallos me, young girl just hatched into childhood. I tend the plastic orphans. An alchemist in a musty root cellar combs blond locks, touches plastic cheeks

in an unspoken language. This tenderness hitched me to hope. If I care for the poor, sick and forgotten, I could also touch the Divine.

Could these whispers of suggestions have Dad's rosary beads praying in his hands, incense singing to me at mass, mysterious pagan baby boxes on my wooden school desk pleading for a coin to ease the unbearable?

Back then these deep longings bubbled up
like a torrential ache, but there
is no reason to hold on to these now,
they have already shaped me.

So many experiences have baked me dear reader. Too many to fashion in this rememory.

Who doesn't remember
their first kiss and who
doesn't remember the
burst like a sparkler
into every part of yourself?

I remember his eyes orbit my face, clear as a morning lake and of course, the gentle smile begging permission to lean in and let speechless lips soak in wild happiness lasting like silent music leaving no physical trace. And who doesn't remember asking why the first shy glance, giddy stroll on rocky beach, a brush of fingers would lead to raptured communion, a slow fire—familiar yet foreign that burns from speaking hearts pulsing in a cubist Picasso. Even if only one kiss and others never followed. It pulled me into a trap all my life—so far and I am caught in a perfect dazzling memory that won't let me go.

I blow wrinkles over my steaming morning tea,
stare at myself in bathroom mirror
I notice how faint lines ripple
along my mouth from habit
of setting my jaw,
pinching my lips against the world.

Douglas MacArthur said that age wrinkles the body, but quitting ages the soul. I think of mom's overstated word, gumption. I was taught to never quit. Seldom did as a kid but I wonder now if my soul is aging because I have quit, said no more, enough already.

Does my aging soul don wrinkles? Naively, I imagine tender lines stroked and kissed like medicine, like cool water. But realistically there are scars of regret and loneliness and loss, lines of enduring forces of every kind from within and without.

I stare at myself in bathroom mirror, touch deep creases between my eyes carefully etched when he makes me laugh so satisfyingly as a luxurious morning yawn. And I have to admit I'm fine with wrinkles, a visual text of my life.

> Don't know if my aging soul has many more years
> Sages say the soul is eternal
> But I want to believe that
> my soul holds lines of verses
> a few more scribbled poems
> a folder of chiseled memoirs
> short story lessons gleaned along the way
> I'm fine with aging
> I'm fine with my wrinkles
> inside and out

A Symphony of Memories*
Geoffrey K. Leigh

A symphony of reflections
cascade across the page
describing experiences, scents
emotional remembrances that
beckon reflections of wild genesis
Aunt May's sweet wine as
trees bend down in a whispering
loving gratitude and
I step into extraordinary wildness
even as I heed Mom's wisdom
walking in the messiness of life
matching Dad's timbre
as he nobly pipered home
tickling the imagination
past networks brought into this moment
a cacophony of experiences
wild tangos with haughty staccatos
scars of regret   loneliness and loss
sharing an orchestration of life's paintings
past connections brought into my presence
bringing intertwined sagas
tears of sorrow and joyous beauty
my marrow vibrates with ruckus giggles
opening my heart, knowing deeply
recognizing the truth that lies underneath
love and hope deep inside me
if I care for the poor, sick and forgotten
nudge hearts from my open door

I also could touch the Divine

A found poem from *Memoir of Loving Gratitude* by Marianne Lyon

Writing Prompts 12

1. What was your favorite story or poem from this collection? Try borrowing some aspect that you liked about that piece and begin writing something in prose, a poem, or a prosetry on a topic or based on an idea that appeals to you.

2. What was your least favorite poem or story from this collection? How would you change the idea to make it more appealing to you? Begin to write something that would improve what you don't like about the piece you identified in the first question.

3. What do your favorite and least favorite pieces tell you about the authors? What does it also tell you about yourself? What do you want to avoid in your preferences of favorite and least favorite topics, issues, and style? Write something about your choices and avoidance in the same piece.

4. Play with writing your own style of prosetry with a topic of your choice.

5. What is a style of writing you never considered before now? Try writing something in that style.

6. What do you like about your new style? What do you dislike about it? Write something about your likes and dislikes.

CHAPTER THIRTEEN

Change

Connection Where?*
Geoffrey K. Leigh

Today we consider love and connection.

Attraction, passion, life's oxytocin. A flower's gentle petals, the pulling at heart strings, songs caressing a meter beat.

Two beings, alive, ecstasy.

What if such seeking is distraction, or even projection of self on other? Connecting by exhale of something inner to another, simply sharing what we do not notice, a sleepy brilliance, awareness long forgotten.

Yet, light within does not wither. But shaded by shadows, absorbed through hurt and pain, contractions. The inner flame burns eternal, a truth, a guide, illumination of path.

Awaken. Your own radiance pioneers you.

* Inspired by Rumi, The Breeze at Dawn

In Search Of The Extraordinary
A Found Play[1]

By Marianne Lyon & Geoffrey K. Leigh

CHARACTERS:

ALBERT: Older, Germanic man with mustache, wild white hair, dressed in 1950s suite

MARY: Older, White woman with silver hear dressed in casual women's clothes

MARTIN: Mid 30s Black man, dressed in a 1960s suite, short dark hair, black mustache

SIDDHĀRTHA: A Nepali man in his 70s, bald, plump, dressed in simple robes.

SETTING & TIME:

SETTING: A forest or natural park with flowers, trees, two paths, and a large rock

TIME: The Present

*   *   *   *   *

[*At rise: SIDDHĀRTHA sits on a rock in traditional meditation posture, eyes closed. MARY enters stage right, sauntering on a path directly in front of the meditator. She carries a small journal and reads out loud.*]

MARY: I want to write something so simple about love and pain, that,

---

1. 1 Much of the dialogue for all four of these characters has been inserted from quotes, poems, or comments said by, published by, or attributed to these four individuals.

even as you are reading, you keep feeling it.

[*MARY looks at nature around the path, spots the meditator, hesitates, then stops completely. As she does so, the meditator opens his eyes and turns his head to look at her.*]

MARY: Oh! Am I disturbing you?

SIDDHĀRTHA: Oh, no. Please, continue on your way.

MARY: I want to wander through this fragrant scenery and take in the joy this lusciousness provides as I construct a poem. Or at least try.

SIDDHĀRTHA: Well, good luck with that, as I'm not so composed with such forms. I simply want to connect in my own manner.

MARY: Of course.

[*MARY turns to look at the tree and flowers to her right and left as she continues to stroll, pulls out her journal and begins to write. She then closes her eyes and takes a deep breath.*]

[*After a moment, SIDDHĀRTHA again opens his eyes.*]

SIDDHĀRTHA: Are you feeling alright? You seem troubled in some way.

MARY: I am.

[*MARY closes her eyes and breathes again, then opens to look at SIDDHĀRTHA.*]

MARY: I always am. I've been watching scenes from the horrible tragedy in Ukraine. People are hurting, suffering, dying. I wish it would stop. It is a serious thing just to be alive on this fresh morning in this broken world.

SIDDHĀRTHA: What a profound expression. Would you repeat that?

MARY: It is a serious thing just to be alive on this fresh morning in this broken world.

[*SIDDHĀRTHA closes his eyes, takes a deep breath, then opens again.*]

SIDDHĀRTHA: I, too, feel extremely sad. That we fight and kill over control of something that is an agreed upon illusion.

[*MARY stares at SIDDHĀRTHA for a moment, then continues.*]

MARY: But an invasion or a war is not an illusion. The death and destruction are horrible. The pain devastating and real.

SIDDHĀRTHA: I agree about the horror of war. Countries certainly are real in our minds, where we hold the construct. But can you inherently see a country's border?

MARY: I can when I walk on the warm sandy Provicetown shore of the Atlantic Ocean.

SIDDHĀRTHA: Yes, (he chuckles). You can see what is defined as the border on the Virginia shore as well. But what about the eastern shore of Panama? And do you actually see a border? Or do you just know it as the edge of that country because we have been taught such agreed upon lines in school geography?

[*ALBERT enters from behind a tree in back center stage, where another path brings him to a convergence with MARY on his right and SIDDHĀRTHA on his left.*]

ALBERT: Actually you could see it, sir, if you were to employ the use of a satellite or Google maps on your iPhone.

[*SIDDHĀRTHA chuckles in response to ALBERT's remark. MARY and ALBERT both smile.*]

SIDDHĀRTHA: Well, I would need your help with either device.

ALBERT: I don't mean to intrude on a conversation. But I'm a bit intrigued by your notion of illusion. By the way, my name is Albert, but not the prince in the can.

SIDDHĀRTHA: Nice to meet you, Albert, not in the can. I'm Siddhārtha.

[*Mary places her right hand over her heart as she speaks, then lowers it.*]

MARY: I'm Mary, as in Mary Oliver. Not the virgin.

SIDDHĀRTHA: Very nice to meet you, Mary Oliver.

MARY: You as well. But I would like to hear more about your elusive perception of illusion.

SIDDHĀRTHA: I don't intend to dismiss the pain and suffering that occurs when people fight and kill each other. There is enough grief and distress in the world without intentionally contributing more.

ALBERT: You say that, but it seems as if you dismiss it by calling it an illusion.

SIDDHĀRTHA: I believe people have a right to choose under what circumstances they want to live. I just mean that we typically come to an agreement of the agreed border we draw on paper, then create signs representing a division in our earth to separate one country from another.

ALBERT: And we invent ways to ascertain those borders, which are important when we insist on defending ourselves from a foreign invader, as Ukraine has been doing when Russian soldiers crossed that line.

MARY: Then it can feel like the world is falling down around us.

[*Mary's hands move out to the side as she finishes. SIDDHĀRTHA places both hands over his heart as he speaks, then returns them to his lap.*]

SIDDHĀRTHA: Oh yes, Mary, which is why we establish rules about how we live and how we separate what is mine and what is yours. Then we fight when we don't agree about what should belong to whom.

MARY: And we hope others will keep their agreement.

ALBERT: While I'm essentially a pacifist, I certainly think it's essential to defend ourselves. For illustration, defense of Ukrainians against Russian invaders, Jews killed by the Third Reich or Armenians by the Turks. Shouldn't we defend people from such cruelty? That's a natural human response and is essential to allow for choices.

SIDDHĀRTHA: It's been a common response for centuries. Does that signify it's the best one? The one we should continue to follow?

ALBERT: I wasn't suggesting that. I believe we should grow and change, learn to do things differently. Yet, we have a difficult time doing so. We still need to defend people against senseless killing.

MARY: Is that why you participated in the letter to President Roosevelt supporting the efforts to beat Germany in building an atomic bomb?

ALBERT: Well, ... yes, ... to some extent. I was worried about Germany developing the bomb because I was sure they would use it. Desperate dictators seem to have little vacillation employing any kind of force to stay in power. And the pressure of a close colleague convinced me to join his efforts.

SIDDHĀRTHA: What was your response after the United States dropped two nuclear bombs on Japan?

ALBERT: It was my worst fear come true. I thought the government's development of such a destructive force would deter more violence.

SIDDHĀRTHA: Many argue over a hundred thousand people died needlessly from those bombs.

ALBERT: If I could take back decisions in retrospect, I certainly would change that one. I have long believed that war is a disease.

MARY: Do you end a disease by continuing to perpetuate it?

ALBERT: No. Yet, I feared the war would end in complete tragedy if my fatherland beat us to the bomb. At the same time, I was wanting to diminish conflicts in my new homeland between Whites and Blacks.

[*MARTIN speaks from the audience but remains seated.*]

MARTIN: Which is why you joined the NAACP and defended Dr. Du Bois when he was indicted for failing to register as a foreign communist agent in 1951.

[*ALBERT brings his hand up to his eyebrows, attempting to see who said that in the audience.*]

ALBERT: Correct, sir. He may have believed in some communist ideas, but he was no agent of a foreign government. And I was willing to testify as a character witness. The judge dropped the charges when he heard I was planning to do that.

[*MARTIN rises as he responds, then walks up onto the stage as he continues.*]

MARTIN: I would too, if I were facing a man who may know how to change gravity in relation to my space and time. (Pause). But more seriously, what about racial injustice in general? Did you raise your voice for that?

ALBERT: No, sir. In retrospect, I should have said more. I did speak out and write articles in support. But I primarily concentrated on my work with limited public speaking. In fact, other scientists were upset that I said as much as I did.

MARTIN: As a side note, my name is MARTIN. I don't mean to accuse you of doing nothing. It's just that we encourage a particular change and let other aspects remain unaltered.

SIDDHĀRTHA: Welcome, Martin. I'm SIDDHĀRTHA, this is MARY, as in Oliver, not the virgin, and that's ALBERT, but not the Prince. As I recall, ALBERT, you were very involved, introducing a change that was important for the time. That's one reason for your Nobel Prize in 1921. You were rethinking physics, not an insignificant task.

MARY: I loved what you said about change, ALBERT. What were your words? I'm getting older and need a refresher.

ALBERT: We can't solve problems by using the same kind of thinking we used when we created them.

MARY: Those words touch me deeply. It's just unfortunate that some politicians don't seem to understand or at least follow your basic concept.

MARTIN: I agree, MARY, both about such touching words and the lack of political understanding by some. We certainly need to change our thinking to change our actions and reactions. But I also think we need to change our hearts. That's what I believe you do when you fashion your words together.

MARY: Thank you, Martin. It helps to heal my own deep wounds.

MARTIN: You continue to look at the bright side rather than the negative, brilliantly expressing your love of nature. The weaving together of keen observations, creative connections, and constant focus on beauty laid the foundation for your 1984 Pulitzer Prize for Poetry.

MARY: I was honored. You, too, were a great catalyst with your own words, pointing out issues and problems as well as motivating courage from your vision of what was possible, believing completely in the transformation of racial injustice. I'm amazed that you, too, remained positive.

[*MARTIN brings his right hand up to his heart until he finishes.*]

MARTIN: I wasn't always that way. I was hateful and angry when unable to play with my best friend at age 6 because I was Black. And again as an adolescent, watching how white people treated my people, hearing about the cruelty, pain and killing of Blacks based on racial prejudice. Not only did the violence and hangings crush my heart, but the vicious words tore my soul. A knife cuts once. Words cut again and again and again, leaving scars few others see.

SIDDHĀRTHA: How did you find any peace from all that?

MARTIN: If my parents had not constantly told me it was my Christian duty to love everyone, I would have had a hard time taking a positive approach.

ALBERT: But such a change I think helped others in your movement who did not have a loving insistence.

MARTIN: I agree. It never is easy. I had to sustain that stance.

MARY: Martin, I understand completely. My childhood sexual trauma made it difficult for many years. It took decades before I could share such painful experiences.

ALBERT: And how did you heal your scars?

MARY: It was the grandeur of nature that helped me brighten my outlook. My constant viewing and writing of beauty, as well as my love for Molly. Such expressions must be made if we are going to survive and live in peace.

SIDDHĀRTHA: It seems the beauty you saw, experienced, and shared touched many lives. Like Albert, I got focused on a major change, wanting to find a way to escape from the trap and cycle of human suffering.

MARTIN: What was the essence of your exploration?

SIDDHĀRTHA: I learned that we can't focus on people's faults. It doesn't help to pay attention to other's omissions and commissions. We must learn to see our own acts, done and undone.

ALBERT: Given your birth into an aristocratic family and walking away from such ease created a major transition in your life. At the same time, you couldn't change the cast system of your people. Every country appears to create some type of separation so one subgroup can feel better than others.

SIDDHĀRTHA: Yes, it's a disappointment that my followers could never completely let go of that judgmental separation. That's my own act undone. My heart weeps for my inability to create such change, both then and later. For it really is not that different now.

ALBERT: I'm afraid not. Read any newspaper, for example. For my fatherland, it was Jews that were blamed for our problems. So people repressed or killed them, as was done to Blacks, Native Americans, Chinese, and others in the United States.

MARTIN: And while I tried to provide leadership in speaking out for Blacks, I had little focus on the status of women. In fact, I insisted my wife remain home with our children. I believed with women getting the right to vote, all would change. I was naive, which my wife, not terribly tactfully, pointed out to me over more than one dinner.

MARY: At least you listened.

MARTIN: Probably more in appearance than fact. Blacks had the right to vote and it didn't change the racism that remained. In fact, it hasn't created equality within this country even today. I got focused on a major change in one area and ignored an important issue in another.

MARY: And women's right to vote hasn't created equality. I think one of the most heinous crimes influential men perpetuate is turning women against ourselves and each other, attacking the whole symbol of creation, simply to maintain their own power.

MARTIN: Not unlike turning Blacks again Blacks, or people of color against one another.

MARY: Yet, with the significant aspects all four of us addressed through our life's work, none of us included a focus on the abuse and trauma that occurs in our families and private homes. I do not intend to sound accusatory. Or dismiss any of your great accomplishments. You, Martin, were also recognized for your life changing efforts by being awarded the Nobel Peace Prize in 1964.

MARTIN: Thank you, MARY. But that doesn't excuse where I failed.

MARY: Agreed, unfortunately. Not one of those changes saved children from physical or sexual trauma in their homes, families, communities, and churches. None of these major issues removed the recurring nightmares of children, myself included, because of such early traumatic experiences.

ALBERT: I remember you writing, "while someone I loved once gave me a box full of darkness, it took me years to understand that this too,

[*ALBERT's hand gestures for Mary to complete the sentence.*]

MARY: ...was a gift in the end. Yet, I would never want to pass it along intentionally.

SIDDHĀRTHA: My dear, Mary, you are so correct. And after all our work, I'm not sure how we make such an essential change. How do we create a life where trauma and suffering are not inherently experienced? How do we modify common and accustomed ways of living?

MARY: Great questions. And none of us produced such an answer.

SIDDHĀRTHA: I continue to meditate on extinguishing the fires of desire, hatred, and ignorance. I wanted to create a world where wise people, like a solid rock, are not affected by praise or blame. Yet, even the us and them judgments of my practitioners limited for a long time any support of female development and achievement.

MARTIN: My admired, Siddhārtha, we all face these challenges. For our lives begin to end the day we become silent about things that matter. And these things matter. It's the silence that keeps cruel acts occurring.

MARY: I believe your words are still true, Siddhārtha, when you said that if we could see the miracle of a single flower clearly, our whole life would change. In essence, my work attempted to help people see that, although I hadn't even read your words at the time. But I believe they point to an important possibility.

MARTIN: And while we may have all come on different ships from various lands, we're all in the same boat now. We must learn to live together as brothers and sisters or perish together as fools. And some days, it seems as if we're simply drilling holes in the boat's bottom. But we could use that miracle now with Ukraine while incorporating greater imagination.

ALBERT: Martin, I agree. I came to think that the true sign of intelligence is not knowledge, but imagination. Curiosity has its own reason for existing.

MARTIN: I didn't read that in the good book. But I think it would have been a useful inclusion.

ALBERT: I keep hoping people don't let their brain interfere with their heart. I think that's what my love of music helped me do throughout my life. Remember, creativity is seeing what others see and thinking what no one else has ever thought. I think our school curriculum needs to be bulging with imagination along with math facts and spelling.

MARY: Profound wisdom, Albert. I desire that whoever you are, no matter how lonely, the work offers itself to your imagination, calls to you like the wild geese, harsh and exciting, over and over announcing your place in the family of things.

SIDDHĀRTHA: Wonderful poetic description, Mary. I, too, think it's important to keep in mind the power of small changes. One moment can change a day, one day can change a life, and one life can change the world. Yet, whatever has the nature of arising has the nature of ceasing.

MARTIN: Sage wisdom, all of it. I appreciate you sharing this today. Still, there remains the question of whether we address more change or keep things as they are; the customary, expected, even habitual.

SIDDHĀRTHA: Change is not easy. But look at where the lack of change has brought us.

MARTIN: Agreed, sir. While the prevalent norms, rules, and patterns may be desired for some, they often are painful for others, as we all have in some way experienced. How do we address that? How do we find a place where all people might experience long life, liberty, and the pursuit of happiness?

SIDDHĀRTHA: I suggest we should find a wise critic to point out our faults, then follow her as you would a guide to hidden treasure. Associate with such a sage. It is the internal change that creates the external manifestation. For if you do not change direction, you may end up where you're headed. But what was it you said, Martin, about being pushed out of the sunlight?

MARTIN: There comes a time when people get tired of being pushed out of the glittering sunlight of life's July and left standing amid the piercing chill of an alpine November. In the end, you can kill the dreamer, but you can't kill the dream. And dreaming is not limited to a sleep. Darkness cannot drive out darkness; only light can do that. Hate cannot drive out hate; only love can do that.

MARY: Only love, only love, only love can do that. It was the core of my life, from which, of course, comes the word for the heart. And, oh, have I mentioned that some of them were men and some were women and some — now carry my revelation with you — were trees. Or places. Or music flying above the names of their makers. Or clouds, or the sun, which was the first, and the best, the most loyal for certain, who looked so faithfully into my eyes, every morning. So I imagine such love of the world — its fervency, its shining, its innocence and hunger to give of itself — I imagine this is how it began.

ALBERT: I agree with all of you. I would only add one more thought from my own work. Just one. You can hold me to that. But it's a long one.

[*ALBERT brings his right hand to his heart for this speech.*]

ALBERT: In a letter to my daughter, I told her
I thought love is the most powerful force that will collide with the current prejudices in the world.

It is the most powerful force that science has not found a formal explanation for.

It is a force that includes and governs all others, and is even behind any phenomenon operating in the universe and has not yet been identified by us.

OK, stick with me here. I promise not to go on forever.

When scientists looked for a theory of the universe, they forgot the most powerful unseen force.

Love is light, that enlightens those who give and receive it.

Love is gravity, because it makes some people feel attracted to others.

Love is power, because it multiplies the best we have and allows humanity not to be extinguished in their blind selfishness.

Love unfolds and reveals.

For love we live and die.

This force explains everything and gives meaning to life.

This is the variable that we have ignored for too long.

Maybe because we are afraid of love. Because it is the only energy in the universe that we have not learned to drive at will.

SIDDHĀRTHA: But who will help us implement this now?

MARTIN: Yes, who indeed.

MARY: We four have tried.

ALBERT: Have given our all.

MARY: In one way or another. And I'm not even a saint.

SIDDHĀRTHA: What more can we do?

ALBERT: Who is left to do more?

[*MARTIN turns towards the audience, followed by the others as each speaks.*]

MARTIN: What about these people out here?

MARY: Our sisters and brothers of life.

ALBERT: Those who can see, who hear. But do you think they would really have something to say? Something unique to contribute?

MARY: I trust you people. I think you could do it.

SIDDHĀRTHA: What say your hearts?

MARTIN: What say your dreams and lives?

ALBERT: I have come to believe that each of us carries within us a small but powerful generator of love whose energy is waiting to be released. When we learn to give and receive this universal energy of love, we will have affirmed that love conquers all, is able to transcend everything and anything, because love is the quintessential power of life. IF we learn to use it that way.

MARY: What I want to say is that the past is past and the present is what our life is, and we are capable of choosing what that will be. So come to the pond, or the river of imagination, or the harbor of your longing. Put your lips to the world and live your life.

About the Authors

Dear Reader/Writer/Poet:

I am a music teacher and world traveler, honored to be named Poet Laureate of Napa County 2021-2023. Verse has always been a part of my life. The older I get the more I am nudged to listen.

A Poem Summons Me

She summons me to converse with her
seeks me out from I don't know where
maybe India's Ganges   Montana Rockies
Words open my eyes   I see myself
Verbs climb me up to jagged top of highest mountain
below my childhood ripples like a stream fed from snowy peak
Her voice is true song of my speechless soul
I feel myself break loose into an abyss
wait for another verse of my life to appear

Marianne Lyon

I taught and conducted social science research in academia for 30 years, writing professional publications that can cure insomnia. It also provided many opportunities to travel nationally and internationally. I moved to Napa Valley in 2010 and now work locally as a customer concierge at David Arthur Vineyards and work on the Yountville Arts Commission.

In collaboration with Marianne, I have composed several short stories that connect with her inspiring poetry for this volume. In the end, I believe life is an opportunity to listen for the internal messages and give them voice, sharing the heartful ideas with others.

Grasping

Clutch safely to the silver pole
Desperately grasping the illusion
Until letting go allows flight
Of love shared through words

In love and gratitude for your interest,
Geoffrey K. Leigh

Also by this author:

Dancing with Audacity: Sourcing Inner Strength. Noussentric Press, 2022. Available through local book stores or on Amazon for print and Apple for ebooks.

Rekindling Our Cosmic Spark: A Noussentric Approach to Living and Parenting. Noussenntric Press, 2017. Available through local book stores or on Amazon.

Printed in the USA
CPSIA information can be obtained
at www.ICGtesting.com
LVHW021807080923
757549LV00001B/107